Raising Teenage Boys

You are Not a Bad Parent -
Secrets to Raising Kind, Confident
and Responsible Boys

Lindsay Moore

Table of Contents

Introduction

I want to thank you for choosing this book, "*Raising Teenage Boys: You are Not a Bad Parent - Secrets to Raising Kind, Confident, and Responsible Boys.*"

Being a parent is perhaps the most rewarding feeling in this world. I remember when my boys were toddlers, but they grew up quite quickly. I have two kids and I certainly love them to bits, but it isn't always easy to parent them. Parenting is becoming increasingly difficult due to various changes in our usual lifestyles and societal norms. Learning to parent a teenage son isn't easy, but it can certainly be accomplished. Trust me, I know and believe this as a parent of a tween and a teen, I often feel a little overwhelmed. After all, he is going through significant life changes. Not only do I need to deal with the changes he undergoes, but I also need to learn to accept the "new" him. It isn't an easy thing for a mother. At times, I catch myself thinking about how quickly he is growing up. Understand that parenthood is a journey. You need to grow along with your child. You cannot treat a teenager the way you would a kid.

Most parents often start to think that they are bad parents if their kid does something wrong. If you have ever thought this, then remove that thought from your mind once and for all. You are not a bad parent. Yes, the way you deal with your kid affects his life. So, it is important that you take on a parenting style that will help you raise kind, confident, and responsible boys. At times, I know how overwhelming or scary it can be to parent a teenage boy. After all, these are the formative years of his life, and the way you parent him will shape his outlook toward life. It might seem like a lot of responsibility for a parent. However, it doesn't have to be. Parenting can be fun, provided you make certain changes to your parenting style.

In this book, you will learn about different aspects of raising a teenage boy, from learning to deal with all the changes you must face, to connecting with a teenager, to help him understand his purpose in life. You must understand that your style of parenting cannot stay constant in this ever-changing world. You will learn about simple and practical tips and strategies you can use while parenting your teenage boys. Parenting a teen doesn't have to be a scary process. A little love, patience, empathy, and conscious effort are all it takes to raise a confident and responsible boy.

So, if you want to learn more, then without further ado, let us get started!

CHAPTER ONE

Being a Parent

B eing a teenager's parent can be tough at times, and parents tend to question their parenting skills. In a bid to be a good parent, parents resort to overparenting. You must understand that being a parent is perhaps the hardest responsibility there is. However, indulging in overparenting does more harm than good. In this section, you will learn about certain signs that suggest that you are overparenting your child. Once you can recognize these signs, you can take corrective action. Apart from this, you will also learn about the common behaviors exhibited by a teenager.

Overparenting Behavior

It is perfectly all right to try and help your children. However, trying to micromanage their lives is referred to as overparenting. Regardless of how good your intentions are, overparenting isn't good. If you constantly hover over your son to ensure that he makes the right choices and try to shield him from the slightest of discomforts, it is a sign of overparenting. Another sign of overprotective behavior is to protect him from fully facing the consequences of his actions. Overparenting is usually the result of a parent's intention to manage their discomfort from seeing their kids stumble and fall. Or it could be because a parent is trying to over-compensate for any guilt the parent feels while disciplining their children. Here are a couple of signs that you are overparenting your son.

Frequent power struggles

Getting into constant power struggles with your kids is a sign of overparenting. For instance, it is okay to force your toddler to eat his vegetables to ensure that he stays healthy. However, if you get into constant power struggles with your teenage son about the way he dresses, styles his hair, or the friends he has is a sign of overparenting. You might have his best intentions at heart, but these things prevent him from finding the independence he is seeking.

Worrying about silly issues

It is okay to be concerned about the safety of your child. However, if you happen to be the only parent who is constantly worried about their teenage son going to school by himself or leaving him alone at home, it isn't right. It might be rather tempting to think that other parents aren't concerned. If you take a moment and think about it, it merely points out that you are over-concerned. If you don't start treating your son like an adult during his teenage years, how will he start acting like one?

Inability to witness their child's failure

No parent likes to see their kids stumble and fall. However, the best way to learn is through experience. If you come to your kid's rescue whenever he faces a slight inconvenience or do not allow him to solve his problems on his own, you are preventing him from learning. If you readily solve all your child's problems, he will never develop the ability to solve any problems he faces in life. Do you remember how your kid used to stumble and fall while learning to walk? Well, in the end, he did learn to walk, didn't he? Keep this in mind and trust that your child will learn.

Prevent the child from making his choices

Usually, parents seem to think that there is a right way to do certain things. However, this kind of thinking enables the parent to micromanage their child's choices. This goes back to the previous point once again. During teenage years, kids seek independence. To be independent, they need to make their own choices. If you force your choices onto him or prevent him from making his own choices, he will only end up resenting you.

Argue with other parents

Another sign of overparenting is getting into constant arguments with other caregivers in your son's life like teachers, other adults, or coaches. For instance, there might have been instances wherein you called up your son's school and demanded that his grade be improved, even when you know he didn't deserve it. Don't try to exert control over how others treat your son. Stop shielding him from the realities of life.

Improper expectations

Having high or extremely low expectations can also be a reason for overparenting. A lot of parents seem to enroll their kids in multiple activities. They do this to the extent that the child has no free time left. From your perspective, it might seem like a good idea since your child is always doing something productive. However, the reality is that you are trying to micromanage the way your child spends his time.

On the other hand, if a parent has extremely low expectations for their child, even that gives rise to overparenting. For instance, you might think that your child cannot do certain things and that you don't even give him a chance to get the work done. You might end up doing his projects or homework for him because you think your child cannot do it. Doing this takes away your child's individuality.

Division of responsibilities

Regardless of the expectations you have about your child, overparenting results in indulging your child. What is the difference between an adult working a job to feed their family and a 5-year old playing in the sandpit? The adult has responsibilities, whereas the toddler doesn't. Likewise, if you want your child to become a responsible adult, you must start giving him age-appropriate responsibilities. Overparenting can result in coddling your son, and this will not prepare him for the challenges of the real world.

Overparenting might make you feel safe and relieve your anxiety about your child's wellbeing; however, it does more harm than good. Don't think that you are a bad parent. Since your intentions are good, you merely need to change your parenting style.

Common Behavior During Teens and Tweens

As the mom of two sons, I know that raising kids isn't always easy. As the child grows older, it becomes difficult. Adolescence is the transitioning time in any child's life from their carefree childhood to the responsibilities of adulthood. This is the phase in a child's life where he will try to portray his maturity and independence. He will face certain obstacles and failures too. All these things are a part of the learning experience but might frustrate him easily. As a parent,

I know how difficult it can be to understand a teenager's behavior. However, there are certain things that almost all adolescents go through as they discover themselves. In this section, you will learn about the common behaviors you can expect from your child as he enters and goes through his adolescence.

Lashing out

You might notice a spike in the incidents where the child is yelling, screaming, or shouting. Also, it might seem like he is lashing out and getting into hurtful arguments. Well, verbal aggression is rather common. Usually, all the hormonal changes he is experiencing when combined with his want for independence results in verbal aggression.

Impulsive behavior

All the hormonal changes and the confusion brought about by teenage years can reduce your son's tolerance levels. Not just this, but his impulse control will be quite low too. A combination of different external factors like peer pressure, bullying, the lack of support at home, economic status, and such only worsens it. So, emotional outbursts are quite common. The next time your son has an emotional outburst, don't shout or yell at him. Instead, try to understand what he is trying to say. Children are impulsive. As the child steps into adolescence, he might be able to think like an adult but doesn't have an adult's impulse control. A combination of these factors means that he will make a lot of poor choices. Low levels of impulse control, when combined with peer pressure, means he will start taking risks. The desire to fit in with others is quite high during adolescence. He might not think things through before acting on his impulses. As a parent, it is your responsibility to correct him when things go wrong and help him get back up on his feet.

Spending more time with peers

A teenager will slowly start to withdraw himself from his family. He would naturally want to spend more time with his peers and don't be offended when your child does the same. It is normal and healthy. However, if you notice that your child is consistently withdrawing from all social interactions, it is time for an intervention. Adolescence brings about a lot of physical changes. Experiencing growth spurts means the teen will start to sleep longer and harder during those times. So, don't be surprised if your teen doesn't want to wake up in the morning or sleeps through the day on weekends. Apart from this, you will also notice that his appetite has increased noticeably. He might want several snacks between his meals. So, stock up the pantry with healthy and wholesome snacks.

Self-conscious about appearance

Apart from this, you will also notice that your teen has become rather conscious about his physical appearance. He might refuse to wear any off-brand clothes and might want to look fashionable. Don't be alarmed by all this. It is quite natural and don't be surprised if he takes a while getting dressed in the morning.

Desire for independence

Your teen will start fighting for his independence. It means that he will try to defy you and push you to your limits. Defiance is quite common. It might certainly frustrate you, but it is a part of growing up. Apart from this, it is quite common for teens to abandon their commitments. He might be interested in playing a sport and after a couple of weeks or months, he might no longer be interested. Don't be surprised, and it is not a reason to panic. He is merely trying to understand what he likes and doesn't. However, you can be concerned if it seems like he isn't interested in anything.

Self-esteem issues

A lot of teens struggle with low levels of self-esteem. The awkward stage of growth and his need to belong are the reasons for this. Your teen neither feels like a kid nor an adult and starts to wonder where he belongs. This can lead to issues with self-esteem. Apart from this, peer pressure can harm his self-esteem too. Regardless of what you want to believe, peer pressure exists and is an undeniable part of growth. Until he learns to rise above it, he needs to learn to manage the same.

Selfish behavior

It is a general belief that teens are selfish. It might feel like all he thinks about is himself, his needs, and his convenience. He might act thoughtlessly and might not even consider the effect his words have on others. All this happens because he is trying to understand himself as a person. Since he is trying so hard to find his place in the world, he will have little or no time to think about others.

Rebellion

Be prepared to encounter several curfew violations. Every teen goes through a rebellious phase where they challenge authority, especially their parent's authority. Teens don't have a good sense of time and often lose track of time when with their peer groups. Don't jump to the conclusion that he is getting into trouble if he misses a few curfews. Usually, the reason is that he merely lost track of time. However, you can certainly set certain limits like asking him to message his whereabouts every hour or two.

Sense of identity

As I have already mentioned, most teens try to get a sense of their identity during adolescence. So, don't be shocked if your kid goes through emo, goth, or any other phase at this time. He might start dressing differently and might indulge in activities he didn't like in the past. Apart from this, he might also struggle with understanding his gender identity or sexual orientation. As a parent, I urge you to talk to your kids about all these things.

Mood swings are common

All the hormonal changes, like changes in the levels of serotonin and dopamine, taking place in his body means that he will be susceptible to mood swings. Don't be surprised if he seems happy one moment and cranky the next. It is normal behavior, and unless the mood swings are rather extreme, it is not a reason to panic.

Want for privacy

His newfound want for independence means he will naturally start seeking more privacy. Respect your teen's privacy and don't go snooping around his room. It is time to start treating him like an adult. You like your privacy, don't you? Likewise, so does your teen. Don't hover over him constantly and give him the space he wants.

Well, now that you know what you can expect during the teenage years, it will become easier to tackle any issues that come up. I am not saying that you can allow your teen to behave the way he wants, especially when such behavior is unreasonable. Instead, I am suggesting that you try to understand him. Once you understand him and feel what he does, it becomes easier to deal with him. You will learn more about all this in the subsequent chapters.

CHAPTER TWO:

Parenting and The Changing World

Changes in Parenting Styles

The availability of information and resources, when combined with the continually changing environment of the modern world, had changed the style of parenting too. In this section, all the different factors responsible for changes in the style of parenting will be discussed.

Parenting style has certainly changed. For instance, take a moment and think about your own childhood. The way you were raised is quite different from the way you are raising your kids today. The style of parenting has not only been changing but has also been developing. The goal of any parent is to ensure the safety and the well-being of their kids, and it hasn't changed. Keeping all things aside, a parent will always be a parent. Change is not only constant but is desirable too. Since everything is changing, family structures have changed too. From modern families to nuclear families, the way individuals are approaching parenthood has also changed. All this is because of progress, a shift in priorities, and open-mindedness. The style of parenting has also undergone a tremendous change. The setup of joint families is a thing of the past these days. Most of the parents find it a little difficult to strike a balance between nurturing their kids and managing their professional lives.

These days, parenting is considered to be a joint venture. There are no predefined roles that a mother, or a father has to play in parenting. The only goal of a parent these days is to help their kids make the most of their lives. Long gone are the days of autocratic style of parenting. Instead, the advancement and progress of this world have led to a more considered approach to parenting. New-age parents believe in guiding their kids in the right direction but without making it seem like an autocratic rule. They are encouraging their kids to be more experimental and open toward all that life has to offer. Parenting has become an active engagement and is changing according to the needs of the kids.

Corporal punishment was quite common, but this has also reduced these days. Instead, parents are coming up with creative ways to curtail their kid's bad behavior. Parenting has undergone a major makeover, and it is mainly because of the awareness of the parents these days. Instead of forcing a kid to do or not do something, parents are taking the time to explain why good behavior is important. Parents have realized that they need to understand their kids, talk to them about their problems, and earn their respect. Once a kid is happy, he will automatically reciprocate. Some believe that the parenting style these days gives kids too much freedom before they are even ready to handle such freedom. Some also claim that parents are under constant pressure to give in to the demands of their kids because of fear of conflict. It can be rather tricky to manage a kid who constantly engages in some form of conflict or the other. In the past, any behavior that wasn't considered to be desirable by the parent would have earned the child some punishment. However, these days, parents aren't resorting to any of those forms of punishment. Instead, they are taking a more positive approach to deal with conflict. Parents today have realized that it is better to explain to the child what they did was wrong instead of merely punishing them.

Relationships these days encourage open and honest communication between parents and kids. All the awareness provided by the media is one of the reasons why parents are quite open to talking about anything and everything with their kids. Talking to kids about sex or their mental health is no longer a taboo subject. Parents are constantly trying to come up with ways in which they can connect with their kids.

The parent-child relationship these days is quite intimate and wonderful. Kids tend to think of their parents as their friends after a certain age. The support offered by parents, coupled with their unconditional love gives kids the necessary confidence to become responsible adults.

Best Parenting Style

A parent's job would be quite easy if kids came along with a certain instruction manual. There have been times when I started wishing for an instruction manual, especially when my kid and I would get into an argument over something incredibly petty or trivial. Well, kids don't come with a set of instructions, and you will need to figure things out as you go along. There are several styles of parenting, and there isn't one method that will fit the needs of all parents. Each style of parenting has a different effect on the child.

The perfect style of parenting would be a method that works well with the characteristics of the child as well as the parent. As long as there is no clash in these characteristics, the parent-child relationship will go on smoothly. A good style of parenting provides sufficient flexibility to meet the needs of the kid while giving the parents some control in the relationship. Here are the different types of parenting styles.

Authoritarian style

This style of parenting usually promotes the "Because I said so" approach. Any parent who follows this style tends to implement extremely strict rules and equally strict consequences for disobeying those rules. If a kid does something wrong, instead of correcting them and explaining things to them, the parent usually believes in punishing the child. Such parents express their love only when their kid does something satisfactory or meets their expectations. This kind of parenting usually helps establish clear and precise limits, rules, and expectations. It does help make the kids more obedient but isn't ideal for all children. For instance, an extremely outgoing child might feel suffocated due to this form of parenting.

Also, this form of parenting tends to remove any traces of independence and self-reliance. Because these kids are so used to being told what to do, they lose their identity. They effectively agree with everything their parent says or does. It is believed that adopting an authoritarian approach to parenting can cause anxiety and depression in kids.

Authoritative style

It might sound quite similar to the previous style of parenting, but it isn't. Parents following this approach tend to set rules and certain limits the same way authoritarian parents too. However, the difference is that in this method, parents tend to explain the logic and reasoning as to why those rules exist. Also, they are willing to put in the effort to understand their child when they have any feedback or objections to the rules. It is a common practice in this method of parenting for a parent to follow along with the child while setting the rules. Whenever a child meets his parents' expectations, the same is rewarded with positive reinforcement. This method is more progressive than the previous approach.

Permissive parenting

This style of parenting doesn't require the parent to set any clear boundaries or rules. The parents tend to be rather loving and nurturing, without any boundaries. Since there are no clear expectations set, a child is seldom punished for bad behavior. Anyone who follows this approach thinks of themselves as the kid's friend instead of the parent. You can be your child's friend, but you must not parent them. This form of parenting can make a child extremely independent, but with little or no discipline. Also, children who are subjected to this form of parenting often tend to struggle with expressing powerful emotions or even dealing with them.

Overprotective parenting

Parents want their kids to be safe and care for their overall well-being. However, overprotective parents tend to take things a step too far. They are overly cautious of all the things that the kids do. A parent's instinct to protect the child makes them indulge in overparenting. Constantly hovering over the child to make sure that he makes the right decisions or preventing him from fully understanding the consequences of his actions are signs of overprotective parenting. Children who are subjected to this form of parenting often find it difficult to become independent.

Uninvolved parents

As the name suggests, these parents are fairly uninvolved in their child's life. They're quite detached from them for decades at times. This form of parenting is usually the result of a parent who is too involved in their own lives to the extent that they have no time for their children. Such parents don't set any rules or consequences for the breaking of those rules. It is a form of neglectful parenting. You need to be involved in your child's life if you want a relationship with your child in the future. An uninvolved parent barely has any interest or time for their kids. In this case, a child is raising themselves.

Well, these are all the different forms of parenting, and most often, the best form of parenting is one that combines all these styles. As long as the parenting approach you opt for works for you and your kid, it is all good. The parent-child equation is one of the most precious relationships one can ever have, and it is important to nurture this relationship. If the style of parenting that you opt for hurts this equation, then it is time to change it. So, it is quintessential that you stay flexible while parenting your kid. All kids are different, and one approach that works for one child might not work for your own kid. Experiment with different styles and see which one works best for you. Also, don't forget to take your child's feedback. Listen to him and ask him what he needs from you as a parent. Another thing that you must keep in mind is that you need to change your parenting style as your kid grows older. You cannot treat a teenager the way you treat your toddler. You need to learn to give your child the freedom that he needs to grow.

CHAPTER THREE:

Differences between Boys and Girls

There are certain differences between the ways boys and girls develop during their teenage years. There is no perfect style of parenting, and you must find one that meets your child's requirements. In this section, you will learn about all these topics.

One day, I was at the park, and one of my friends asked me, "Is it easier to raise boys or girls?" Well, I never really gave this question much thought before. After all, kids are kids regardless of their gender. Some people tend to believe that it is easier to raise boys, whereas some believe it is easier to raise girls. As a mother, I think what is important is to concentrate on raising the child regardless of his or her gender. Kids are kids, and they are still humans, after all. Maybe it is about societal conditioning. However, there is one thing which is true, boys are different from girls. The way you decide to raise your kid is entirely up to you and is not dependent on their gender.

As long as your parenting approach works for you as well as your kid, you are in the clear. It is sad to see that the society that we live in has somehow managed to stereotype each gender. Some parents tend to believe in engaging their kids in gender specific activities. For instance, I have seen a lot of parents push their kids into dancing or baking lessons because they're a girl. On the other hand, there are also those parents who make their boys play sports because it's a manly activity. Why does parenting have to be defined by gender norms?

Don't let any archaic gender norms define your style of parenting. You need to do what is right for your child. If your boy likes to dance, then what is the harm in making him join a dance class? If he likes sports, allow him to play sports. Allow your kid to do what he likes as long as it doesn't harm him.

Besides, there are certain differences between boys and girls. No, I'm not talking about physical differences. There are certain cognitive and behavioral differences between boys and girls. The first difference is related to the development of the brain and especially the rate of this development. However, there is another factor that needs to be taken into consideration while a child becomes an adolescent because parents raise their kids differently. Well, it is time that we all accept that we do raise boys and girls a little differently while they are growing up. For instance, when a girl takes her first steps, it is a parent's instinctive behavior to coddle or protect her from stumbling. Whereas, if the baby is a boy, it is more likely that the parent will encourage him to be rough. So, it is safe to say that parental influence does play a significant role in the developmental differences portrayed by boys and girls.

I find it rather surprising that a lot of parents seem to have this misconception that boys don't listen to anyone. This got me thinking about whether it is a genetic difference or parental influence. It isn't fair to stereotype an entire gender by saying, "Boys are stubborn." Well, I think it is all about the way you parent the child. Your child's behavior will predominantly depend on your parenting style.

Researchers seem to believe that the hearing ability of boys is not as finely attuned as that of girls. The hearing ability of a girl develops quicker than that of a boy. While our boys hearing might be at a normal level by the time he enters elementary school, it will still not be as finely tuned as a girl's. It essentially refers to the range of hearing. This genetic factor is one of the reasons why boys tend to need more discipline and a hands-on approach to learning than girls. Also, another thing I've noticed is that a parent might not hesitate to drag their boy by the hand but will hesitate to do the same to a girl.

A lot of the differences between both genders comes down to development. The developmental process in boys is usually slower than that of girls. Boys tend to take a while longer to develop speech skills when compared to girls. So, a lot of these differences boil down to basic genetics. Now keeping the mental development aside let us talk about physical development. Physical development in boys tends to be quicker than in girls. Girls tend to mature quicker than boys hormonally and mentally. Basic biology combined with parental influence causes developmental differences between boys and girls.

Gender differences are slowly disappearing these days. However, they still exist. For instance, boys are encouraged to run as fast as they can or swim as far as they can. Boys are expected to succeed and earn their living. The unfair societal conditioning suggests that a man is supposed to support his household. However, it is time that we put all these gender-oriented norms to rest. Normally, parents tend to find it easier to let go of their boys than their little girls. Why does society expect this of a boy and not from a girl? Boys and girls are equally capable of doing everything.

Another major difference between boys and girls comes in the aspect of communication. Gender stereotyping has led us to believe that girls tend to be overdramatic or talk too much. However, this might be associated with biology once again; girls tend to start talking earlier than boys. Girls are often encouraged to start talking from an early age, whereas a lot of parents prefer it when the boys don't talk much. All these archaic expectations and stereotypes aren't doing this generation any good. It is time to forget about societal conditioning and start doing what is right by your child.

Most of the differences between boys and girls aren't about gender anymore. If you go through history, you will realize that what kids are taught is just a major throwback to all the archaic ideas which existed in the ancient world. Understand that this world that we live in is rapidly changing. The ideals that might have been true decades ago aren't true anymore. As a parent, your focus must be on raising a competent and responsible child. He must be able to fend for himself and lead a successful life. So, forget about gender differences, forget about the question of boys versus girls, and instead focus on your kid. The right style of parenting is the one that works for you and your kids. The best method of parenting is the one that enables your child to lead a responsible and successful life.

Well, teenage years can be a testing time for a kid as well as his parents. All parents often think that their parents had it easy with them and that they are having a hard time with their own children. However, if you take a moment and think about all the risky behaviors you indulged in when you were a teen, you will realize that history is just beating itself. Every generation seems to think that the previous generation had it easy. As a parent, you will want to protect your child from any frustrations or even disappointments that you might have experienced as a child yourself. You cannot do this. The harder you try to do this, the more difficult you're going to make it for your child to grow up. As a parent, you must be able to give your child the necessary support and guidance to steer him into adulthood with minimal difficulties. Be prepared for your teen is going to crash and burn at times. However, you can help soften this blow. You can work on a parenting style that will help your kid.

CHAPTER FOUR:

Changes in Your Son

The transition from a child to a teenager can be tricky. The common cognitive, emotional, psychological changes that your son might undergo during his transition to becoming a teenager are discussed in this section.

Common Changes when Boys Transition into Teenagers

Adolescence can be a bumpy ride for not just the parents, but the kids too. However, you can reduce this turbulence. If you try to understand the changes your kid goes through and the challenges that you might have to face, you can work through all obstacles that come your way. One of the rather dramatic phases of development that your son will go through is adolescence. During this phase, he tends to become fully aware of the developmental process. Understand that your son can watch and experience the changes taking place and has to accept the same. Your child will undergo several physical, cognitive, social, and personality changes during his teenage years. Phew, that's a lot for anyone to take in! While he is undergoing these changes, he also needs to accept these new changes. Coming to terms with all this might not always be a pleasant experience for him. You can help him along the way if you are aware of the changes he will undergo. Here are certain changes that your boy might experience while transitioning into his teenage years.

While transitioning from tween to teenage years, your child undergoes a lot of changes. These changes are a rather big deal for him. Kids tend to face certain bumps during their teenage years. The level of physical maturation they undergo influences the extent of these bumps. For instance, social awkwardness can be caused if he matures earlier or later than his peers. Also, puberty tends to cause certain awkwardness in the relationship shared between a child and his parents.

Experiencing growth spurts, developing facial hair for the first time, significant hormonal changes not only affect the child but the parents too. On top of everything, the constant worry of having to measure up to the impossible ideal of the perfect physique propagated by social media further pressurizes the child. Believe it or not, your child is constantly worrying about being under or overweight, being too hairy, and so on.

Did you know that once your child hits their teenage years, different areas of his brain start to develop rapidly? As a result, by the time he is between 15 to 16 years old, he can use logic and reason the way an adult does. However, the portion of the brain, which is responsible for planning and thinking ahead needs a while to develop. This is primarily the reason why a lot of teens tend to make poor decisions, especially when it comes to taking risks, using alcohol, engaging in sexual activities, and any other risky behavior. Essentially, a part of his brain can think and act like an adult, whereas the other part cannot. Your son might be able to understand the logic behind why a certain thing is right or wrong, but his brain isn't fully mature enough to grasp the consequences of such actions. A teenager's brain undergoes certain cognitive developments, but it isn't fully matured yet. The changes that he undergoes can cause turbulence in a parent-son relationship.

A change, regardless of how desirable it is, isn't always easy. When a child enters his adolescence, he is trying to understand who he is. It is often referred to as an identity crisis. It isn't a bad thing, but it isn't always a comfortable transition. It might not sound like much to an adult, but during their teenage years, a child needs to make a lot of decisions. He needs to decide who he wants to be in life, what his morality is, his temperament, his sexuality, opinions about politics, and so on. Apart from this, he also needs to make career-related decisions. That's a lot to take in and can be a source of enormous stress. This process of self-discovery isn't easy and can cause tension in their personal relationships.

There are several social changes, but the most significant of all is when the child develops his independence. Some teens start exhibiting signs of independence earlier than others. However, almost all teens will start spending less time with their parents at this point. They start to feel quite comfortable and secure with their friends or their peers more than their families. Also, this is the time when they start forming rather complicated relationships. Sexual attraction and dating have become quite common. His hierarchy of preferences tends to change when it comes to relationships. Don't be surprised if your son seems to want to spend more time with his peers or partners. This change can also be another reason for conflict.

The two major challenges which you will face as a teenager changes are independence and communication. You must learn to deal with his push for independence and learn to communicate even when he seems unwilling to. It is not surprising to note that teenagers often want to do things earlier than what the parents deem as being appropriate. This applies to everything from the way he dresses, to owning a phone, following curfews, or even going out with his friends. Everything will become a negotiation where he will try to assert his sense of independence.

He might not wish to discuss his life with you, and don't be offended by this. It is a very common change that all teens go through. Most parents might find this rather disconcerting, but by learning to communicate with him, you can overcome this obstacle. As a parent, you might feel a little neglected or even rejected. You might start to think that your child no longer loves you or needs you. However, this is merely a face when he is trying to discover himself. You will learn more about communicating and connecting with your teenager in the subsequent chapters.

CHAPTER FIVE:

Psychology Involved

U nderstanding the psychology of the parents and your teenage son will give you a better idea about parenting. It will give you the insight necessary to understand your growing teen. In this section, you will learn about the psychology of the parents as well as their teenage boys.

Psychology of a Teenage Boy

It is often believed that teenage boys are full of angst. However, once you delve into the psyche of a teenage boy, you will realize that they experience a myriad of emotions. It is quintessential that you understand what he experiences if you want to learn to parent him. Teenage boys certainly bring about a lot of changes with them. Your kid is trying to come to terms with the fact that he is no longer a boy and is now headed toward becoming a man. Teens tend to give the impression that they are often frustrated, uncertain about themselves, and stressed out. However, you must consider the fact that they are undergoing major physical, emotional, and cognitive changes during their teenage years. This is a major overhaul for your teen too. Therefore, it is not surprising that they feel uncertain.

I often wonder what turned my once sweet and innocent child into an impulsive, risk-taking teenager. I am sure that even you wonder about this. Well, the answer to this lies in the allotment of the brain. The common traits that a teen exhibits like exasperating the adults, indulging in impulsive behavior, showing poor judgment, and social anxiety are all related to the teen's biology. Even stubbornness and rebellious attitude can be related to their changing biology.

You might clearly present certain arguments and lay down certain thoughts in front of your teen, which make perfect sense to you. However, it is not a good idea to assume that your teen perceives all of this the same way that you do. As mentioned, the brain undergoes a major overhaul during the teenage years. When this happens, the behavior and thought process of your teen changes too. For instance, a teenager might drive his car too fast around a curve and crash into a lamppost. He might have seen the speed limit signs, undergone the necessary tests to obtain his license, and heard all the driver's safety tips given to him by spirits. Even after all this, he somehow managed to act without thinking and crashed his car. Well, all this goes back to the way his brain is developing.

The white matter that is present in the brain's frontal cortex is responsible for all his poor judgments. Decision-making, the ability to decide, making judgments, and impulse control are all associated with the frontal cortex. The white matter microstructure relays the signals between the grey matter and the neurons. During the teenage years, white matter starts to form, and the unnecessary grey matter disappears. Well, all this sounds too complicated. Here is a simple example for you to get a better understanding of how your teen's brain works.

Think of all the neural pathways as electrical wiring. The bare or live wire is dangerous. It needs some degree of insulation. Insulation helps to protect the wires while improving its ability to relay signals. So, the more insulation there is, the better the signals will be relayed from one point to another. Since this insulation starts to form in the teenage years, it can be one of the reasons why a teenage boy behaves impulsively. Not everything can be blamed on biology, but denying this relationship is not a good idea.

Well, enough with the technical stuff. Let us look at some simple things that your teen keeps thinking about. Being a guy is certainly not an easy task. We all live in a society, which has conditioned us to believe that men have to be tough. Your son is trying to find his place in the world while trying to live up to this unrealistic expectation. This can be a source of immense stress for him. Apart from this, he needs to deal with peer pressure too.

All teens go through an awkward phase. Your son might be going through this phase at the moment. He might have started to experience certain things, physically as well as emotionally, which he hadn't in the past. This is a lot to take in. Often, it tends to overwhelm teens and make them feel uncertain about themselves.

Apart from this, he can be worried about rejection and might be insecure about himself. We all live in a world that's dominated by social media. From the time he wakes up in the morning until he goes to sleep at night, he is surrounded by social media. Social media is helpful, but it often propagates unrealistic expectations of how people should look or how they must live their lives. So, your teen might feel insecure that he doesn't belong in this oh-so-perfect life. Well, it can be rather tough.

He also has to come to terms with the reality of the way life works. He might have imagined that his life would unfold in a certain manner. This might not happen, and it can be a source of frustration for your teen. He is also trying quite hard to find his place in the world. The need to be accepted by his peers and finding his identity are quite real for your teen. Apart from this, they start becoming quite conscious about the way they look. The body starts to change, facial hair starts to grow, and all these things can certainly make him feel conscious. This is especially true if he is maturing at an age which is faster or slower than that of his peers.

Well, that's a lot of stress that your teen is facing. Understand that his brain hasn't fully accepted all of this yet. If he's acting out or lashing out, it is mainly because of his inability to come to terms with all of this. As a parent, you must understand that he is facing all of this. If you want to connect with him or want to form a close bond with him, then you must try to understand him. Try to recall your teenage years, the awkwardness you went through, or the uncertainty you felt. I'm sure you also experienced all these things. Then why is it surprising to know that your teen is undergoing the same? So, parents, take a step back and try to see the world from your teen's perspective.

Psychology of Parents of a Teenage Boy

All the changes that come along with adolescence are not just hard for the adolescent but for the parent too. Most of the tension can be reduced when the parent starts to understand why the child behaves the way he does. I've noticed that a lot of parents with young kids tend to be filled with a sense of dread when they realize that they have to deal with a teenager soon. Teenagers are risk-takers because they don't have a sense of judgment to understand the consequences of their actions or words. They will also try to push away from their parents or even family members. They prefer to be in the company of their peers and others their age. Teenagers can become rather difficult to communicate with and show signs of rebellion. Parents can start to feel that they're being rejected by their teenage kids, and this can be rather hard for the parent.

I remember all the times when I felt neglected, helpless, and even worried about how to treat this new person my son was becoming. I'm sure you might have experienced these emotions along with some infuriation or annoyance as well. Your child's refusal to follow your rules or spend time with you can make you miss the child that he was until a couple of years ago. These things might be true, but you need to understand that your child is growing up. Teenage years can be a wonderful time too if you change your perspective towards it. For instance, your teenage son could be full of energy, enthusiasm, and wide-eyed amazement at all the possibilities that the world has to offer. He will start showing signs of empathy that a toddler doesn't. During this time, he will start thinking like an adult. It means that you have a greater chance of connecting with your child at an adult-like level. Apart from all this, you can take a moment to appreciate the person your child is becoming.

When the tween years come to an end, your child enters teenage years, and after a couple of years, he comes out an adult. However, this progression from adolescence to adulthood can be turbulent. In this section, we'll learn about the different things that a parent feels, that you feel when your child enters his teenage years.

Direction in life

Parents tend to go through certain adjustments of their own too while their kids go through teenage years. They are also trying to come to terms with all the changes that the teen is going through and are trying to cope with it. At this stage, parents tend to realize the fragility of their age while their kid is still very young. A mother is almost at the end of her childbearing years, whereas her kid is just entering those years. You might realize those different avenues in life which were once open to you are no longer available. Whereas, new opportunities are opening up for your child. There is almost a sense of irony to all of this. It is normal for a parent to experience a sense of uncertainty or even envy. Don't think of yourself as a bad parent if you're jealous of all that your child has which you no longer do. It is merely a part of growing up. Yes, it is a phase of growth for the parent too.

Grappling with reality

From late-night feedings, to the time your son took his first steps, to the first day of school, to him becoming a man. This is a lot for a parent to take in. Coming to terms with the reality that your child is no longer the toddler that he once was is not an easy change. You need to come to terms with the reality of the person that your teenage son is becoming. You might have had an image of your extremely popular and extroverted child in your mind. However, in reality, your child is an introvert who likes to keep to himself. Or perhaps, you've had a vision that your son is an academic virtuoso, but he has an inclination towards arts and sports instead of academics. As a parent, you might experience feelings of disappoint ment or even frustration that your teenage boy is nothing like what you imagined in your head. Well, reality often differs from what we visualize it to be. It is essential that you come to terms with all these changes and accept your son for whom he truly is.

Style of discipline

You must set certain ground rules along with the consequences of breaking those rules. These rules must be non-negotiable. However, it is time that you take a different approach towards discipline and your teenage son. You might not feel that your child is ready for all the freedom available in the world. However, it is not for you to decide. You might feel scared that you can no longer protect your little one. However, it is time to understand that he is no longer a child and is on his way to becoming a man. You cannot try to discipline an adult the way you would discipline a kid. For instance, as a tween, his curfew might have been 9 pm. Now, he is no longer a tween and is a teenager. So, it is time to renegotiate this rule. Don't try to be too fix upon certain ideas you have in your head about what he should and shouldn't be doing. Instead, treat him as an equal and talk to him about the changes that he would like. By doing this, you both can come up with a list of rules and regulations. Perhaps you can ask him to come up with the consequences of breaking those rules too. Doing this will make him feel like an adult and at the same time, make him realize the fact that abandoning responsibilities comes with consequences.

Time to let go

You cannot micromanage your child's life or schedule. It is time to realize that you need to let go. It is not an easy task for a parent to let go of their son. To be fair, you have been, or rather he's been an integral part of your life so far. I remember when my son started pulling away. I too felt a little sad that he no longer needed me. Well, understand that he is just carving out independence. It doesn't mean that he stops needing you. It just means that he's exploring his life. Give him the freedom to explore his life and shape his reality for himself. The harder you try to hold onto him, the more resistance he will put up.

Staying connected

I know it feels like your child is pulling away from you. It does become a little tricky to stay connected with your teenager. However, there are ways in which you can do this. Don't be disheartened if he doesn't want to spend as much time with you as he did in the past. Instead of feeling bad, you can come up with different ways in which you can stay connected with him. You will learn more about this in the subsequent chapters.

Acknowledging his sexuality

As your teen is coming to terms with his sexuality, it is time for you to embrace the same. You need to find ways in which you can accept and also deal with the sexual choices your teen makes. If your child feels like you don't support him, he will withdraw. Instead, show him that you love him unconditionally, regardless of his sexual orientation. You will learn more about dealing with uncomfortable topics like sexuality in the subsequent chapters.

CHAPTER SIX:

Advice for Parents

Parenting Mistakes to Avoid

I must admit that there have been times when I felt rather frustrated and even slightly hurt while dealing with my teenage boys. I'm certain that all other parents might have also experienced this at some point or another. In my bid to be a better parent, I might have unknowingly done things that strained my relationship with my boys. In this section, let us look at certain common parenting mistakes that must be avoided while dealing with teenagers.

If you want your bond to stay strong, then you need to make certain changes to your parenting style. While talking to your teenage son, do you ever talk to him as if he was still a child? It's not only about what you're saying, but the way you talk too. You need to understand that your child is moving towards adulthood. If you keep talking to him as if he's still a child, it will only frustrate him more. Even if you don't agree with what he is saying, it is important to start treating him like an adult and listen to what he's saying. Everyone wants to be heard, and your son wants the same. Parents often complain that it feels as though their child doesn't respect them. Well, respect is a two-way street. If you treat your teenager with respect, then he will reciprocate.

Do you ever treat a conversation with your son like it is an obligation or a chore you need to complete? If yes, then he can perceive this, and he will be hurt. Understand that he is no longer a child but is maturing into an adult. I don't mean that you must not occasionally lecture your child or focus on his behavior. Instead, ensure that a majority of your conversations are about connecting with him and forming a bond.

Most parents tend to multitask while talking to their kids. However, try your best to avoid this. If your son is talking to you and your multitasking, it sends a message that what he's saying isn't that important. You're inadvertently conveying that he doesn't deserve your full attention. So, the next time you're talking to your teenage son, ensure that you give him your undivided attention.

At times, parents tend to try too hard. Don't try to force a conversation and let it flow naturally. Also, ensure that you don't interrupt your son while he is talking. Let him finish, and then you can talk.

Dealing with a Teen

You might not realize it, but your teen's behavior is also related to the way you parent him. Maintaining a good relationship with your teen will help him feel happier and more content with life. In this section, you will learn about simple tips that will come in handy while dealing with your kids. These tips are practical and easy to follow. Also, they will help reduce any conflicts or tension too.

Be a parent as well as a friend

A common mistake that a lot of parents make is that they are either a strict parent or a close friend to their teens. However, you must find a middle ground. All teens desire to be understood by their parents, appreciated by them, and loved for who they are. Not just this, but they also desire a lot of independence and freedom. Don't think that by being a friend, your teen will not respect you. Don't you cherish and respect your friends? It is about establishing healthy boundaries. It is about being a good parent and a friend to your teen. Make the atmosphere in the home conducive of healthy discussions. Create an environment where your teen can talk to you about all his worries.

Spend time together

You need to spend at least a couple of minutes every day talking to your teen. It doesn't have to be about anything specific. Just check in on your teen and ask him how his day was and if he is fine. You can set up a small routine. Maybe you can talk to him for a couple of minutes before he goes to sleep every night or talk to him once he is back from school. It is merely a way of staying in touch with your teen. Also, it encourages him to start talking about what's going on in his life.

Appropriate parenting

If you don't want to or refuse to acknowledge the fact that your son is growing up, it will only invite conflict. Understand that he is growing and that his needs will change. Your son will naturally want more freedom. However, this doesn't mean that you have to be scared about asking him where he's going or whom he's going out with. It is a good idea to get to know your son's friends and parents too. Don't be hesitant in asking for these details. However, while doing this, ensure that you don't indulge in over-parenting. Don't be a hovering parent and instead give him his freedom. You can certainly set certain restrictions on that freedom, provided that they are reasonable. If they are reasonable, then your son will comply with them.

Manage your expectations

Your son will obviously want to be his best self. As a parent, it is your duty to ensure that he can do this. You need to support your child in his endeavor to be his best self. However, this doesn't mean that you start setting goals that you want him to accomplish. Instead, work along with your teen and try to understand what he wants. Once you understand this, it becomes easier to set goals that he can work toward. Try to support your teen. Even if you don't understand what he wants right away, spend some time with him, talk to him, and you will soon understand. Remember that your teen is seeking your approval; even his behavior doesn't convey this. So, if you set unrealistic expectations for him, he might be scared that he will disappoint you. All this will only frustrate him and make him feel anxious.

Mealtime

Make it a point that you have at least one meal with your son daily. It can be breakfast or dinner. As long as you both share a meal, it gives you the perfect opportunity to open up communication. Try to make it a point that you eat as many meals together as a family as you possibly can. This will certainly have a positive effect on the way your teen feels about himself and his family. If he can see the family as one unit, he will feel more secure and relaxed. Also, this is a perfect way to unwind and stay in touch with the happenings of each other's lives.

Communication is quintessential

It is important to keep the lines of communication with your teen clear and open at all times. He must not be scared to talk to you about things. However, at the same time, he must not take this liberty for granted. You need to get down to his level and talk to him as his peers would, while being a good parent. Learning to communicate efficiently and effectively will help reduce the chances of any miscommunication. Also, it will help strengthen your relationship. You will learn more about communicating and connecting with your teen in the subsequent chapters.

Don't ignore self-care

Leading by example is a great way to go about parenting a teen. If you live a healthy life and your teen sees you doing the same, it might give him the inspiration to follow in your footsteps. Make sure that you get plenty of sleep, eat a balanced diet, and do things that make you happy. When your teen sees you do all of this, he will naturally be inclined to do the same. By promoting self-care, your teen will start to feel better about himself.

Independence

Yes, your teen will want a lot of independence. However, don't try to push independence on him if he is not ready yet. Some teens take a while longer to step out of the nest. It is okay. Don't push him into anything that he is scared of. Be there to nurture and guide him. Allow your teen to understand that you are there for him.

By following these simple steps, you can certainly improve the relationship you share with your teen.

CHAPTER SEVEN:

Connect and Communicate Effectively

E ffective and efficient communication is essential to maintain a healthy relationship. In this section, you will learn about how you can connect and communicate with your teenage son.

Steps to Connect with a Teenage Son

As my son started inching towards adolescence, I became abundantly aware of how our relationship was changing. I realized that he was no longer interested in following me around like he used to. It was surprising that he didn't want to share as many details about his life as he used to. I still remember when he came home after his first day of elementary school and was excited to talk about all the new things he had experienced. While, when he started high school, I noticed that he was withdrawing himself more. If I could manage to get a complete sentence from him insofar as a shrug or a grunt as a response, I started to feel lucky. I was tired of hearing "I don't know," and "whatever" as responses.

I started to miss all the times that we spent reading books together and cuddling when he was a little boy. I knew that he needed his space and that for him to grow up he required independence. However, the mother in me could not accept that I was unable to connect with my son. It is quite difficult when he starts to pull away. A lot of parents simply give up because they don't know what to do. Let me tell you a little secret, you can always connect with your son regardless of his age. In this section, you will learn about certain things you can do to stay connected with your son.

Understand him

Try to get to know him and understand what really matters to him. You can ask him questions but don't be nosy and don't try to pry. A simple question that you can ask your son is, "What is bothering you?" I am sure that he will open up if not immediately, then eventually. Ask him how school is going on and about his friends. Try to get to know his friends. Learn about the kind of music he likes or the food he relishes. Try to be open and curious about the things he likes. Once he notices that you are making an effort, he will reciprocate. Ask him about the things he likes and doesn't. If you don't agree with something that he likes, then instead of writing it off, try to see it from his perspective. If you are unable to do this, then ask him why he likes what he does. Try to get him to start talking and you will be able to find common ground.

A little special treatment

You can do something that is just for him and it will show that you love him. At times, a little reminder that you are there for him and that you love him is necessary. It can be something as simple as cooking something that he loves. This is all it takes to reconnect with your teenage son. Make his favorite meal, sit down with him, and talk to him. Try to be more involved in the kind of activities that he likes.

Validation matters

Understand that he is going through a challenging and crazy time in his life. He will need his space at times, so give it to him. It isn't just you who is facing challenges. Your teenage son is torn between desiring independence and needing you. Have faith, even if it looks like he's pulling away right now, he will come back. However, for this to happen you need to make a conscious effort. Be mindful of the way you talk to him.

Don't engage in any power struggles and let go of all petty arguments. Your son might say hurtful things in the heat of the moment but holding onto those words will only hurt you. If you have a problem, then wait for him to calm down, and then you can talk to him about it. Don't restrict his choices, and instead let him decide. He does see your approval and validation. If he seems genuinely excited about something and you don't clearly understand it, then try to understand it. Try to validate his feelings and don't make him feel like they don't matter.

Plan a fun activity

A simple way to connect with your teenage son is to do something fun together. It can be something as simple as sending him funny texts or memes. If you come across something that you think he will enjoy, share it with him. Make it a point to engage in some fun activities together. Maybe you can create a playlist together and watch a movie. Do something that you both enjoy, and it will give you a chance to bond. There are plenty of things you can do together!

Let him choose

Allow him to choose and give him a chance to be the expert. If you're struggling with the latest gizmo or need some technical help, then ask him. The feeling of being helpful to one's parents can be quite enriching for a child. Maybe you can both listen to a podcast or watch a video together. Even if it doesn't interest you, try to do something with him. It gives you a chance to talk about the things that he likes and get involved in his life.

Getting something done together

Maybe you can do something together. It can be something as simple as going out for a haircut together. Regardless of the haircut he chooses, don't react negatively to it. You're trying to reconnect with your child and strengthen the bond you have. So, it is important to allow him to understand that you are there for him. You can ask him for his help with grocery shopping or offer to do any other activity that you like. If he allows you to, then maybe you can help him organize his room. Don't start nagging, criticizing, or lecturing him while doing any of these things. If you don't agree with something, then ask him to explain it from his perspective. While he is doing this, ensure that you're carefully listening to him. The way your child thinks will certainly be quite different from the way you think.

Essentially, the idea is to spend as much time with him as you possibly can. All these ideas might not work for you, but something will; it's a process of trial and error. Keep trying different activities with different approaches until you find one that clicks.

Tips to Establish Efficient Communication

Communicating with a teenage boy might seem like an art at times. The good news is, you can learn to do this. In this section, you will learn about the different tips you can follow to establish effective communication with your teenage son.

There exists an undeniable connection between anger and hunger. So, a simple thing to do is make sure that neither of you is hungry before starting a serious conversation. Making sure that his sugar level is stable will prevent the chances of any grouchiness. Also, when he is well fed, his ability to engage in conversation and stay focused improves.

It is a good idea to notify him in advance about the topic as well as the time when you plan to talk to him. Don't expect him to go into the conversation with a list of points or counterpoints that he wants to make. However, it does give him some time to think about the things you want to talk about. It allows him to present his thoughts and ideas in a clear manner. Not just that, it also gives you some time to think about the things you want to talk about.

If you want to converse with your child, then forget about lecturing him. If you talk to him in a condescending tone or start lecturing him, then it will certainly put an end to a discussion. The chances of the discussion escalating into an argument are quite high when you start lecturing your child. Instead of lecturing him, it is a good idea to keep things brief. Just get to the point and talk to him about the topic at hand. Also, the chances of miscommunication increase when you start beating around the bush instead of getting to the point.

Apart from this, it also increases the chances of your son zoning out while you're talking. You must learn to manage your emotions. Don't allow them to get the best of you. Your son might say or do things to trigger you, but don't give in to the urge to react. Instead, learn to respond carefully. You can diffuse even the tensest of situations by responding calmly. You cannot control the way your son thinks or behaves. However, you can control the way you respond to all these things.

Boys tend to think better when they are active or are engaged in some sort of movement. So, you can start talking while walking or doing something else. If you force him to sit down and then engage in a conversation, it just makes the whole thing seem rather forced and formal. Instead of doing all this, it is a good idea to go on a walk with your son and then talk to him about something. Also, the chances of reacting violently tend to decrease when you are engaged in a physical movement.

At times, it is better to communicate indirectly. If you constantly stare down your son while having a rather important conversation, then it can make him feel threatened or suggest aggressive behavior on your part. You don't want to come across as being aggressive while having an important discussion. So, I suggest that you have certain conversations while walking side-by-side or even while driving. The best way to have an important discussion is to only occasionally make eye contact. This will make your son feel calm and relaxed. The more relaxed he is, the more open he will be about communicating.

You can guide him and tell him when he does wrong. However, stop yourself from patronizing him. If he feels like he doesn't have any power, then it will merely trigger his fight or flight response. The feeling of helplessness can effectively end the conversation. For instance, instead of telling him what he needs to do, you can ask him what you can do to help him. Or perhaps you can ask him what his plan of action is to accomplish what he wants. Also, never assume anything while talking to your son. When you assume things, it not only increases the chances of miscommunication, but also puts him on the spot. For instance, you can ask him if he's dating anyone instead of asking him whether or not he has a girlfriend. By keeping things general, you make it easier for him to open up to you.

It is not just about talking but it's also about being a good listener. If your son feels like you're not listening to him, then he will immediately clamp up. This is something you want to avoid. So, don't interrupt him while he's talking and actively listen to him. Ask follow-up questions to show that you have been listening to him. When he feels like he's heard he will want to talk to you more often. Instead of judging or telling him that he's wrong, ask him what he feels. Take a moment to listen to him and carefully analyze what he's told you, and then think of a positive way in which you can respond. We all like to be heard and the same stands true for your son too. So, be a good listener.

It might not always be easy to understand what he says. At times, you might even be against his ideas or thoughts. However, try to see things from his perspective. Instead of putting him down, ask him to explain things to you. Show him that you are curious about what he thinks and that you're willing to understand his perspective. Doing this is not only respectful towards him but will encourage him to talk to you more. Also, it increases the chances of him responding in a respectful and pleasant manner. Try to keep a neutral perspective on the topic at hand. Don't formulate opinions or jump to any conclusions. Wait for your son to finish his piece and then talk to him about it.

People say things when they are hurt, angry, or frustrated. Give your son a little leeway. If you are hurt by something he has said or done, then talk to him about it once he has calmed down. Keep reminding him that you are there for him and that you will support him. If he sees encouragement and uncondi-tional support, then he will want to be more involved with you. He needs to understand that he can depend on you, and that he isn't alone.

There will be certain topics that your child will not want to discuss with you. It is bound to happen and is natural. Don't force him to talk about something that he clearly doesn't want to share with you. When he is ready, he will share with you. However, for this to happen, you need to show that you love and support him. Only when he feels like you will keep an open mind, will he come and talk to you about it. Don't let it bother you, if he doesn't want to share something. Remember that when he is ready, he will come to you. Don't push to talk about something. If you do this, you are merely pushing him away. Perhaps, your teen is comfortable talking about this to someone else or maybe one of his peers. If that's the case, then let it be so.

By following these simple steps, you can ensure that you're able to communicate effectively and efficiently with your teenage son. So, the next time you're talking to him, make sure that you follow at least some of these steps. Do this for a while, and you will see a positive improvement in the relationship you share.

CHAPTER EIGHT:

Learning to Manage Emotions and Conflict

L earning to resolve conflicts and manage your emotions without losing control of the situation is quite important. Especially when you are dealing with a teenager, conflicts are quite common, and if left unchecked, they can ruin your relationship. In this section, you will learn not only about how to manage any conflicts with your son but also how to manage your emotions in stressful circumstances.

A clash in opinions is bound to happen as your child grows older. The way he thinks, and his opinions will change with age. It is quite normal to disagree, but you need to manage the disagreement constructively. You need to learn to deal with conflict and prevent it from escalating into a nasty argument. When you start managing your emotions and conflicts, you are setting a good example for your son to follow.

What is the purpose of conflict management? It is quite normal to clash with your child as he enters his teenage years. In fact, expect these clashes to happen more often. For instance, you might disagree about your son's choice of clothing or the way he spends his time. Conflict is not only normal, but it is healthy too. This shows that your child is able to think for himself and is becoming an independent adult. Remember that no two individuals think alike. So, you cannot expect your child to always think like you. However, too much conflict is also undesirable. It not only increases tension in the household, but it also puts stress on your relationship.

If you can effectively deal with conflict, you can strengthen your relationship with your son and also reduce the stress levels in the house. Also, by effectively dealing with conflict, you are showing your son an important life skill. You must understand that you need to pick your battles carefully. It is not worth getting into a conflict over a petty issue. So, even if you don't like your child's latest hairstyle or disapprove of his friend circle, don't engage in a conflict. Instead, take a minute to think about whether it is actually worth arguing over. You can save all this energy and use it for an important discussion in the future.

Tips for Getting Ready for a Conflict

As mentioned, conflicts are unavoidable. In this section, you will learn about certain tips that will help you constructively deal with conflict.

You were a teenager too once, and do you remember those days? Take a moment and think about your teenage years. A little self-introspection can help get a better understanding of what your child is feeling. When you do this, it reduces the chances of any unnecessary conflict. It can maybe give you insight into what your child thinks or feels. All this will help you relate to your child in a better manner.

In the previous chapters, you were introduced to the psychology of a teenage boy. Keep in mind that your son's brain isn't fully developed yet. It cannot think and grasp things the way you do. His perspective is still limited. Keep all these things in mind while engaging in conflict with your son. He might not be able to see the risks or consequences of his actions, which you are able to see. He might be incapable of seeing things from your perspective.

When you realize this, you can take steps to make things clearer for him and easier to understand. Try to step down to his level and talk to him. At times, it might not be easy to make him see things the way you want, but this doesn't mean you need to fight about it. All things can be solved with communication. So, make sure that you keep the channels of communication open and clear at all times.

As mentioned, pick your battles wisely. That means you need to be a little flexible while dealing with petty issues. When you show a little leniency and flexibility, it encourages your son to reciprocate. It might also convince him to listen to you. A combination of these factors means that you will be able to discuss things without engaging in any conflict.

At times, you might lose your cool. It is bound to happen. So, don't expect perfection from yourself or demand perfection from your son. After all, you're both humans. So, be easy on yourself and your son too. Don't lose self-control and don't give in to the urge to overreact. Learn to say sorry and apologize when you are wrong. Accepting your mistakes only makes you human and doesn't diminish you in your son's eyes.

Whenever you are angry, upset, or even frustrated while engaging in any conflicts with your son, you might harshly react. Instead of hurting him by saying something you didn't mean to, take some time to compose yourself. Once you are calm, you can talk about the issues at hand. Apart from this, take some time and think about what you want to say. Think about the words you want to use and concentrate on the tone while you're talking.

Another tip is to ensure that most of your conversations are about serious issues. If all you talk about are difficult topics, then your child will lose interest. Keep things pleasant and casual as much as you can.

Spend time with each other and enjoy each other's company. Do things together and strengthen the bond you share with your son.

Tips for Effective Communication in a Conflict

In this section, you will learn about certain tips that you can keep in mind while you're communicating with your son in a tense situation.

You need to learn to stay cool, calm, and composed. Don't try to multitask while in an argument. Maintain a little bit of eye contact, listen to your kid, and treat him the way you would treat an adult. If you want him to respect you, then you need to respect him. It is a two-way street, after all.

You must allow your child to speak his mind. If you keep interrupting him or don't allow him to say what he thinks, he will feel frustrated. All this will only escalate the conflict and diffuse it. So, give him a chance to share his point of view. Once he is done talking, then you can talk. After all, there is no rush.

Start being open about what you feel. Don't try to suppress your feelings. If you do this, sooner or later you will end up having an outburst. Also, start expressing yourself. When you express yourself, it enables your child to understand where you are coming from. Instead of telling him he's not supposed to do something, tell him what you feel when he does it. Explaining this can change the way he views a situation. For instance, if you feel uncomfortable that your son keeps staying out quite late at night then instead of grounding him, talk to him about it.

Express your concerns for his safety. When you do this, he will stop thinking of you as a disciplinarian and will start seeing you as a concerned parent. Give him a brief explanation of your view and make it clear that his well-being is your priority. Instead of asking him not to hang out with certain friends, you can talk to him about how you're worried about his safety. Maybe you can ask him to tell you whom he's going out with and where. This is a reasonable way to deal with conflict.

In a conflict, you must be prepared for some form of negotiation. You cannot always be firm or strict and expect your child to comply. If he starts feeling that regardless of what he says or does, you will not change your mind, then he will stop expressing himself. This will certainly end any potential conversations too. It is okay to discipline your child when he is wrong, but there must be scope for negotiation too.

When you display your willingness to compromise, you are teaching him a valuable life skill. For instance, your child might be adamant about purchasing the latest game. You might not want to indulge him because you think it will interfere with his academics. Instead of denying this from him, you can come to a mutually favorable agreement. You can tell him that you will purchase the game for him provided he agrees to study for an hour or two every day. You can set a condition that you will take this game away if his grades suffer.

Try to keep your calm while saying no. Show your disagreement with something in a respectful and calm manner. For instance, if your child wants to get a piercing and you don't agree with it, convey the matter calmly. Instead of telling him no, you can say something like, "You are only 14, and you have plenty of time in your life to get a piercing. So, for now, the answer is no."

By following these simple steps, you can diffuse tension even in conflict.

Dealing with the Aftermath

At times, conflict is unavoidable even after your best efforts. Engaging in a conflict is emotionally draining, not just for you, but for your kid too. The way you deal with the aftermath of the conflict is as important as dealing with the conflict. I remember feeling rather heartbroken after a heated exchange I had with my son one time. In the heat of the moment, we both said certain hurtful things to each other. I know that I didn't mean anything I said and neither did he. However, things were said that I now regret. Instead of obsessing over the argument, I took steps to ensure that we spoke about our feelings later.

Once we were both calm, we spoke about the hurtful words that were exchanged. Therefore, I believe that it is quintessential to learn to deal with the aftermath of the conflict. In this section, you will learn about a couple of practical tips you can follow to ensure that there is no unpleasantness after a conflict.

It might take your child a while to calm down after a conflict. It is normal for your child to feel disappointed or even hurt if you said no to something that he wanted. You can encourage your child to calm down by calming yourself down first. Once you do this, you can show him that you understand what he is saying but that you cannot agree to it at the moment. Also, give him a chance to express himself. If he is disappointed, let him express this. Or if he needs space and time then give it to him. Give him the space he needs to re-analyze his thoughts and calm down. If you push him, then he will rebel.

If you are having a difficult time calming down after a conflict, then it is time for some self-introspection. If this doesn't help, then you can talk to your partner, loved one, or anyone you trust. Explain the conflict to that person and ask for their opinion. Don't try to prove yourself right or your child wrong here. The idea is to resolve the conflict and maintain a positive environment in the household. Self-care is quite important. Also, at times, seeking someone else's opinion can also help put things into perspective.

Also, be vigilant when your child starts deflecting conflicts. At times your kid might prevent conflict by lying to you or doing things behind your back. If you want to have an open and honest relationship with your child, then be prepared to be mindful of your feelings as well as reactions. If your child notices that you keep reacting unfavorably to the things he says or does, then he will clamp up.

Managing Anger

One thing that you must always remember is that a teenager is still learning how to express himself and his emotions. At times, your child might think that he needs to express his opinions rather strongly for you to listen to him. Also, understand that he is still learning how to deal with any stronger powerful emotions he feels. If you are engaging in a conflict with your teenager, then you need to learn to deal with his anger too. In this section, you will learn about a couple of simple tips you can use to keep your emotions in check while dealing with an angry child.

If you know that your child is angry, then you need to stay calm. If you want to prevent the conflict from escalating, then one of you has to keep your calm. It is highly unlikely that your teen will be the one to keep calm. As a parent and an adult, you must stay calm regardless of what your child says in anger.

If you feel like it is becoming increasingly difficult to keep your composure, then disengage. Try to physically remove yourself from the situation if possible. Take a break and let things simmer down before you carry on with the conflict again. A small break of even six seconds can help you re-analyze the situation.

You must not only listen to what your son is saying right now, but you must also let him understand that you are listening. By simply nodding your head, you can convey that you are listening. Now is not the time to multitask. Show your son that he is the center of your focus at present. Let him know that you not only care about the things he's saying, but you also understand what he's saying. Once he's done with his angry outburst and is calm, you can start reasoning with him.

Always stick to the issue at hand. Don't deviate from the topic or combine any other issues. Don't bring up any issues from the past. By bringing up the past, you're not doing yourself or your child any favors. It will only add fuel to the fire.

Once you have done all of these things and your child has calmed down, it is alright for you to express yourself. You can take some time, compose yourself, and start talking about what you feel or what your fears are. Try to keep this as simple and precise as you possibly can. If this talk becomes too long, then it will sound like a lecture or a monologue to your child, then he will soon be disinterested. After all of this, it is time to reach a mutually acceptable decision. If you notice that your child is feeling upset about something that you said or by the way you spoke to him, then you need to apologize. Regardless of whether you are right or wrong, if you have hurt him, accept the responsibility. Assure him that it will not be repeated again.

CHAPTER NINE:

Deal with Uncomfortable Topics

There are certain "talks" a parent must have with their teenage sons, and some of these talks can be rather uncomfortable. In this section, you will learn about a couple of ways in which you can have important discussions with your son about sex and mental health. These are two important topics that you must not avoid or ignore.

The "Talk" About Sex and Sexual Health

One of the most awkward conversations that a parent can have with their kids is about sex and sexual health. However, it is quintessential that you don't avoid this discussion. It's quite likely that your kid already knows about sex, but as an adult, it is your responsibility to start a healthy dialogue about it. Talking about sex is no longer a taboo subject. The media tends to showcase sex in a skewed manner, and this can affect the way kids think about sex. In the past, talking about sex was merely restricted to the basic mechanics of the process. However, these days, you must not only talk about that but also the attitude surrounding sex. Sex is a natural act, and you need to tell your son the same thing.

A lot of kids often feel ashamed talking about sex or their sexuality because of all the stigma that's associated with this topic. However, times are changing, and the way the world perceives sex and sexuality is undergoing a tremendous change. The ideal time to talk to your son about all this is during his teenage years.

The first thing you must do is understand how much your son knows about sex. It is quite likely that he knows a lot more than you would probably want him to. However, you must prepare yourself to listen to what he has to say without being critical or judgmental. If you make him feel uncomfortable about this topic, then you can forget about having a healthy discussion. You need to maintain your composure throughout the discussion if you want him to feel comfortable talking about it. Allow him to talk before you start talking. Once you do this, ask him what he thinks about the way sex has been portrayed by the media, his attitude towards it, and how he feels about it. When you do this, it gives you a basic idea of where to start.

Blame it on societal conditioning or objectification of sex. Most teens tend to think of sex as a conquest and a status symbol. It usually happens because it is portrayed as such in the media these days or because he heard his friends talk about it in that manner. So, the first thing you need to do is work on changing your son's attitude about sex. As a parent, it is your duty to tell him that this is a wrong attitude towards something that is quite natural. Talk to him about his readiness to engage in sexual acts or any sexual intercourse. Tell him that there is no rush and that he can wait for as long as he wants to. Tell him that he doesn't have to feel pressured into doing something he isn't comfortable with. A lot of teens tend to give in to peer pressure and end up having sex before they are even ready for it. Sex is not only a physical act, but it also has certain emotional implications.

Sadly, sexual objectification of women has become the norm of society these days. Take a moment and think about how you would want your son to treat his potential partner. No one must be subjected to sexual objectification, regardless of their gender. Talk to your son about treating his partner as his equal and not as a sexual object. He needs to learn and respect his partner. He must be told that it is not okay to pressurize anyone into having sex or engaging in any sexual activities. The easy access to porn these days tends to give young teens artificial ideas about what sex is and how people behave during sex. Tell him what he sees is not always the reality. Talk to him about the necessity of consent. Teach him that it all comes down to mutual respect.

It is time to talk about porn and reality. People in pornographic videos are actors, and they are doing their job. Ask him not to get any wrong ideas about sex or set any unrealistic expectations of what it's supposed to be like.

This might be a slightly difficult pill to swallow but prepare yourself to accept that your son might have sex before you would want him to. Because of this, it is quintessential that you talk to him about proper preparation. It is also important that you talk about sexual wellness and sexual health. If you have any doubts that your son is engaging in any sexual activities, then talk about sexual health. You can ask him about it, or he might be upfront about it. However, if he doesn't come clean about it, tell him about the necessary precautions he should take to keep himself and his partner safe. Talk about basic contraception like condoms, which he can use to prevent any sexually transmitted infections. Talk about sexually transmitted diseases, how he can contract them, and the symptoms to watch out for. Tell him that he needs to come to you or seek help as and when necessary.

Another thing you must keep in mind while talking about this topic is that you must not pry into his sexual life. Let him talk about it if he wants to. Don't force him, or you will just push him away.

When done at the right time and with the right person, sex can be a beautiful act. So, give him a choice to decide what he wants to do about it. As a parent, it is your responsibility to talk to him about it and help him maintain a positive attitude about it. Engaging in sexual activities is not a status symbol.

The "Talk" About Mental Health

Mental health is as important as physical well-being. If your kid isn't mentally happy, then it will affect the overall quality of his life. These days, awareness of mental health has been steadily increasing. People are no longer worried about being stigmatized about their mental health. Starting a conversation about mental health might not be easy, but you need to ensure that there exists an open dialogue about this topic. In this section, you will learn about a couple of simple tips you can use to talk to your son about his mental health.

You must be genuine. If your teen senses that you are faking it, then he might not want to talk about the issue. Keep in mind that he knows when you are being genuine. If you do feel uncomfortable talking about this topic to him, then be upfront about it. For instance, you can say something like, "I am not entirely sure how to go about this topic," or "Talking about this topic isn't easy for me." By being honest, you are opening up doors for open communication.

In your attempt to try and connect with your teen, you might want to use some slang that you usually don't.

If you're thinking about it or have done something like this in the past, stop doing it immediately. Don't use any slang or any other words that you usually wouldn't. Try to talk to him the way you normally speak. Don't create any unnecessary hoopla about this topic. Mental health is a very delicate subject, and you need to approach it tactfully.

Do you ever struggle to express yourself? I'm sure you do, and it's the same for your teen too. When you struggle to express yourself, don't you need a moment or two to regain your composure? A moment of silence can help your teen put his thoughts into words. Allow for some silence. It isn't necessarily a bad thing. If you notice that your son is struggling to express himself, then give him a couple of minutes to get his thoughts together. Also, don't interrupt him. If you do this, you are effectively preventing him from formulating his thoughts into words.

The setting for this type of conversation matters as much as the conversation itself. Where and when you want to talk about this topic will influence how comfortable your child feels. For instance, if you are in a noisy place and try to have this discussion, like a coffee shop, then it will defeat its purpose. You must ensure that you and your child are both comfortable in the setting. So, opt for a quiet place if you want to talk about this, like at home, or go to a beautiful park or even sit outdoors. Again, avoid doing anything else while talking about your child's mental health. It's important to give them your full undivided attention.

You must not only give your son a chance to explain himself, but you must also understand where he's coming from. Do not trivialize any emotions or feelings he's expressing. To him, this is quite serious, and if you ridicule or trivialize it, he will not want to discuss it any further. Doing this will convey to him that his feelings or emotions don't matter. Having a conversation about these things will get more comfortable, the more normal you make it.

CHAPTER TEN:

Help your Son Find His Purpose

Teenagers often feel lost and unmotivated. In this section, you will learn about practical steps you can follow to ensure that you can help your son find his purpose.

What Makes a Teen Feel Lost?

Teens tend to feel demotivated or even lost at times. It is quite normal. As a parent, you have to help motivate your teenager. In this section, you will learn about the primary reasons that make a teen feel lost.

Worrying about failure

We all tend to worry about failure and are also quite scared of it too. The same stands true for your teen as well. Worrying about all the things that could go wrong and how he could at any moment feel lost is totally normal. A lot of kids tend to enter their teenage years with unrealistic expectations of what life will be like. Well, the reality is often less than ideal when compared to their idealistic scenarios. For instance, your son might have been used to getting good grades and is now obsessed with perfectionism. So, he naturally develops the fear that if he doesn't excel, he will be treated as a failure. He is not only worried about disappointing himself, but he is concerned about disappointing others too. This can cause an immense amount of mental stress.

Indulging their inner critic

We all have an inner critic who continually criticizes everything we do or say. This inner critic can also induce self-doubt. However, most of us are good at ignoring this tiny voice in our head. If your teen starts indulging in their inner critic, he will soon be overwrought with self-doubt. This self-doubt can effectively prevent him from leading a happy and fulfilling life. Also, if your teen is regularly subjected to criticism by his parents, family members, peers, or even teachers, this fuels his self-doubt. Apart from this, if he engages in any negative thinking about himself, he will feel lost.

Anger

Teenagers are inherently moody because of all the physiological changes they experience during adolescence. For instance, your son might not want to do his schoolwork because he is upset with his teacher. Or he might not want to go out with his friends because of a spat they had. Anger can effectively prevent him from being happy. Teenage angst is a sensitive issue. Until your teen finds a reasonable way to channel his rage, it will hamper his life.

Teens are often uncertain about where they stand in this world. During these years, they tend to continually struggle to find their own identity and discover their purpose. This certainly isn't an easy journey. However, you can help them along the way and ease their stress.

Steps to Motivate a Teenager

Well, now that you are aware of the reasons why your teen seems to be demotivated, it is time to remedy this situation. At times, when parents try to motivate their kids, it comes across as nagging. If your child feels like you are nagging him, then you will never succeed in motivating him. You might think that scaring, commanding, threatening, warning, or even lecturing can help motivate him. In this section, you will learn about a couple of simple strategies you can use to help motivate him.

Value addition

What is the value addition that your teen will get for doing something? "What is in it for me?" This is a common question any teen will ask themselves when they are asked to do something. If your child doesn't understand what he stands to gain from doing something, then it will become quite challenging to motivate him to carry out a task. A lot of teens feel rather insignificant and are constantly trying to prove their worth. If your kid understands the value of the task, then he will be inclined to do it. For instance, your teen would be somewhat motivated to take on a part-time job if it helps him save up for a car he wants. Likewise, if you can show him that doing a particular task will add value to his life, there is a greater chance that he will want to do it.

It's his choice

The inclination of your teen wanting to do something will increase if he has a say in it. If he feels like he is being forced to do something, then he will resist. If you go with the old, "Because I said so" approach, it will certainly backfire. Instead, sit with your teen and determine the list of tasks he must complete and the timeframe for each task. Allow him to set the consequences along with some expectations. For instance, if your teen is entrusted with doing all the laundry once a week, then allow him to go about it the way he wants. Don't try to micromanage. If he wants to do the laundry at night, then let him. Give him the responsibility and the power to act, if you're going to delegate any work.

Failure to remember

At times, the lack of motivation is the reason why your teenager hasn't done anything. It's most likely because he forgot. Teens usually have a lot of things going on in their lives, and this means they can forget certain tasks. So, as a parent, you must try to get your teen more organized. Explain the importance of organization and how it will help him in life. Once your teen understands what he can get from being organized, he will be more inclined to do so. Also, you can work along with your teen and create a schedule or a timetable.

It must be attainable

If the goals that you have set for your teen or the goals he set for himself are unattainable, then he will be demotivated. Setting unrealistic goals is a recipe for disaster. If you want your teen to be motivated, then you need to help him set realistic and attainable goals. Also, there must be certain small goals that he can achieve. Once he attains a small goal, it automatically gives him the motivation to keep going. At times, kids tend to put off a task merely because it looks overwhelming to them. So, if you start dividing up a task into smaller and more attainable tasks, it will be easier for him to complete them.

Incentives are helpful

This goes back to the first point. It always helps to spell out what your teen stands to gain by doing something. However, at times, he will need to do certain things even when there isn't an obvious incentive attached to it. For instance, he needs to do his homework merely because it is important for his academic record. However, there are certain tasks for which you can easily provide him an incentive. For instance, if you know that your teen isn't naturally athletic, then you can provide him an incentive if he takes up a sport. Or if you know that your teen tends to leave things half-done, then you can offer an incentive upon the completion of a task. By providing incentives, you are motivating him to keep going. While setting the incentives, you can consult with your teen. The incentives don't have to be anything big. It can be something as simple as an extra hour of TV time or maybe an extension of his curfew.

It must be fun

If your teen likes what he is doing, then he will be naturally motivated to keep at it. You would obviously want to spend more time doing something if you enjoyed it. The same rule applies to your kid too. For instance, if you want your kid to improve his scores at school, then come up with interactive or fun activities that can help him learn. There are several educational apps and games you can use to do this.

Motivating your teen to do better in life is your responsibility. Once your teen gets into the habit of doing better, he will not require any assistance.

CHAPTER ELEVEN:

Promoting Independence

Independence is quintessential. A child is used to depending on his parents for support and guidance. However, once he enters his teenage years, he needs to become independent. Independence isn't restricted to the way he dresses or how late he stays out. Independence is about being able to do things by himself. Some kids are inherently independent, while others need a slight push. In this section, you will learn about a couple of simple strategies you can use to help your child become more independent.

The Need for Independence for a Teen

Attaining independence is quintessential for a teenager's journey to adulthood. To do this, your teen needs certain freedom to try out new things and have new experiences. However, this doesn't mean that he will not need your support or assistance from time to time.

What does the term independence mean to a teen? Usually, a teen is said to be independent when he no longer has to depend on his parents and is capable of taking on more responsibilities. An independent teen is capable of solving problems by himself and making decisions. Also, an independent teen has a sense of his identity. However, it is quite normal for parents and kids to disagree on what independence means to them. Usually, this disagreement stems from the degree of independence, which needs to be granted to the kid. As a parent, it is quite natural that you worry about your child's well-being. You might worry that if you give your child a lot of freedom at a young age it will encourage them to indulge in risky behavior. Some parents then will shelter their kids. However, by doing so, you are effectively taking away your child's need to be independent.

Do you remember learning to ride a bike when you were a kid? I'm sure you did not get it right on the first try. You might have fallen off a couple of times or even stumbled. Eventually, you did manage to learn. Naturally, your kid will also make mistakes. However, remember that this is a part of the learning process. Experience is the best teacher there is, and by encouraging him to be independent, you are equipping him with one of the most important life skills.

It is quintessential that you learn to maintain a balance between your concerns as a parent and your child's need for independence. A simple way to go about doing this is by ensuring that you both share a positive and healthy relationship. Ensure that your kid can calmly talk to you about anything. Keep in mind that a teenager is still trying to figure what life holds in store for them. It isn't necessary that he always knows where he's headed. So, you and your kid will both learn ways to strike a balance between each other's needs as you go along. There isn't a scientific formula to help you understand how to maintain this equilibrium.

How to Promote Independence in the Teenage Years

However, there are certain things that you can do to help your child become independent during his teenage years.

Unconditional love

The first thing that you must do is ensure that your child knows that you will always love and support him. Unconditional love and support can work wonders for one's confidence. When he knows that he can always count and depend on you, it will give him the courage to move towards an independent existence. It will enable him to discover himself and what he wants to do in life. The simplest way to show that you care for your child is by saying, "I love you." You can start showing interest in the things that he likes or paying attention to him when he talks. Apart from this, you can also show your support for him by giving him some privacy.

Respecting his opinions

It is quintessential that you start respecting his feelings as well as opinions. All the changes brought about by teenage years can be overwhelming for your kid. If you can understand his feelings, you will be more empathetic towards him. He will certainly pick up on this empathy. He will become independent if you start treating him like an adult. To do this, you need to take his opinions and ideas seriously. When he feels like he is valued, and his opinions matter, it will improve his self-esteem. Self-esteem and confidence will help him become an independent adult. You and your child don't have to agree on a lot of things, and disagreements are bound to pop up. It might not be easy for you to handle this, but you need to try. Your child will find his place in this world because of the opinions he has. So, start respecting them regardless of whether you agree with him or not. Even if you have any disagreements, handle them calmly and politely.

Family rules are important

You must set certain ground rules that are common for all the family members. The rules you set must be applicable to communication, and general behavior. These rules will enable your kid to understand what is and isn't acceptable behavior. It also helps him understand what you expect of him and reduces the chances of any misunderstandings. Apart from this, it also encourages parents to dole out consistent treatment to their kids. Once you make these rules, ensure that you enforce them consistently. Also, keep these rules flexible. Certain rules will need to change as the child grows older. As your child grows older, ensure that you get him involved by altering the rules or setting any consequences for breaking the rules. Don't be too lenient or too strict while setting these rules. They essentially are guidelines that will help your child become independent in the future.

Age appropriate treatment

Every teenage boy thinks he is ready to be an adult. However, one thing that they all fail to realize is that adulthood comes with a ton of responsibilities. So, don't be surprised that your 13-year-old starts to think of himself as a responsible adult. Although, you can start encouraging him to be more responsible by allowing him to make certain decisions for himself. Start treating him according to his age. Giving him too many or too little responsibilities will hamper his transition to be a responsible adult.

Encourage decision-making

You can introduce your child to a problem-solving approach whenever he needs to make a decision. Doing this, will help instill a sense of independence in him.

Here are the steps that you need to follow for a problem-solving approach.

- Discover the different options which are available;
- Carefully weigh the pros and cons of each of these options;
- Think about the course of action if the plan doesn't work (have a backup plan); and
- Tell your child how you think he handled the situation.

Try to include him whenever you're making any family decisions. This will make him feel like his suggestions and opinions matter. If there are any major decisions that a child needs to make, then don't make it for him. Instead, make these decisions along with him. For instance, if he is thinking about going to a specific college, then don't decide whether the institution is good or bad for him. Instead, weigh in all the options along with him and decide which route will be the best option for him. Remember that your kid is still learning about impulse control and might not be capable of making the best decisions all the time. However, by slowly encouraging him and giving him the liberty to decide, you are improving his decision-making ability.

Exercising his independence

Make it a point to provide your child with a couple of different opportunities wherein he can exercise his newfound independence. However, make sure that all these situations are risk-free and will not harm the well-being of your child. For instance, you can give him the opportunity to decide whether he wants to learn a new skill or perhaps a new sport. You can encourage him to take on any positive risks that you know will pay off. You can also encourage him to take on a part-time job once he is of appropriate age. Taking on a part-time job will give him a sense of independence and will also give him a taste of adult life.

However, as much as your child desires his independence, letting go of him will not be easy. I remember the time when I realized that my little boy is no longer dependent on me and is becoming a responsible adult. It is a rather bittersweet realization. On one hand I was incredibly proud of him, and on the other, I was missing the little boy he once was. As your child is discovering his independence, be prepared for certain power struggles. You need to learn to manage any conflicts that come along the way.

CHAPTER TWELVE:

Dealing with Addictions

The modern world is full of different things that can become quite addictive. This section deals with modern-day addictions your teen might be exposed to and the ways to help him overcome them.

Modern-Day Addictions

You might have already had a talk with your kids about drug and alcohol abuse. However, did you talk to them about the different modern-day addictions? Whenever someone talks about addiction, the first thing that might pop into your head is drugs, alcohol, or cigarette dependency. However, these are not the only forms of addiction that your teen is exposed to these days. Not all addictions need to be based on chemical dependency.

The world has certainly developed, and so have the kinds of addictions. There are different things that a teen can get hooked onto which go beyond the regular addictions that you might think of. For instance, dependence on social networking, prescription drugs, texting, and sex have become the most common forms of addiction these years. Yes, children are addicted to these things.

Before we start discussing these things, it is essential to understand what addiction means. Addiction is a disorder wherein an individual begins to engage in compulsive behavior to reap instant gratification regardless of the dire consequences associated with it. Essentially, addiction is a disorder. When you call someone an addict, you are essentially talking about his or her dependency on a behavior or a thing.

The advent of social networking has certainly revolutionized the world that we live in. Social networking has made it easy for us to stay in touch with each other, regardless of where one lives. It certainly has its perks, but it also has certain potential side effects. Social networking can be very addictive. Social networking platforms like Facebook, Instagram, Tumblr, Twitter, and Snapchat are quite addictive. They are either constantly posting on these sites or are checking their feed multiple times a day. It has come to a point where a teen starts to feel like he's missing out on something if they don't regularly check their feed.

If your teen spends all his time on these platforms, he is missing out on creating a social life for himself in the real world. Spending too much time in the virtual world is not a good thing for anyone. If you notice that your teen is addicted to any of these social networking sites, then it is important that you take corrective action. For instance, you can set a daily limit to the time that he spends on these platforms. You can start getting him engaged in other activities to distract his mind from social networking.

The abuse of prescription drugs has also become quite common these days. This problem has almost become an epidemic. The abuse of prescription drugs not only creates drug dependency but also harms the overall well-being of an individual. It is important to educate yourself about the abuse of prescription drugs. The recent statistics about the abuse of prescription drugs is rather alarming. Did you know that over 2,500 teenagers abuse prescription drugs for the first time every day ("Protect Your Kids," 2010)? Well, that is quite scary. Therefore, it is time to acknowledge that dependency on prescription drugs is quite real. A lot of teens tend to do this because of peer pressure or merely because they're experimenting. So, be a vigilant parent and take remedial action immediately.

Teens certainly love to spend a lot of their time on their latest smartphones. The addiction to texting might not seem dangerous. However, if you take a moment and think about it, it in fact affects their overall productivity. If your kid is constantly on his phone, he is missing out on life and the things going on around him. Spending too much time on smartphones is hampering the ability to do anything else. Teens often feel frustrated when they do get an immediate response and tend to drive themselves crazy thinking about all the possible reasons why the other person hasn't replied. A cellphone is a great way to stay in touch with your kid, regardless of where they are. However, you need to supervise the amount of time your kid spends on it. For instance, the other day, I noticed that my son spent three hours doing very basic schoolwork, which he could've completed in less than 30 minutes, had he not spent all his time texting. Teens are usually always on their phones regardless of where they are or what they are doing.

Teenagers certainly have to deal with a lot of hormonal changes during this stage in their life. However, this generation seems to be a little too interested in indulging their sexual urges. It is perfectly all right for people to engage in sex or sexual activities. However, one must not create a dependency for it. Sex and sexuality seem to be the latest form of addiction these days. One of the reasons why this is happening is because of easy access to pornography. It is okay to be curious about sex. In fact, it is quite healthy to have a curious and open mind about it. But the real trouble starts when a teen starts to form an obsession around this. More and more kids seem to be engrossed with engaging in sexually explicit behaviors. Different apps, like Tinder or Bumble, have made it quite easy for people to find sexual partners. No longer does a person have to go through a couple months of courtship before engaging in sexual activities. Long gone are those days. Now, all that you need to do is download an app, and voila, you have a willing partner.

These addictions have become rather rampant these days. Most of these start as harmless indulgences that become obsessive over time. If you notice any of these behaviors in your teen, then it is time that you take action. You must help him overcome these addictions.

Tips to Help Your Son Overcome These Addictions

Whenever a parent learns that their teen is addicted to something, the first reaction is that of shock and disappointment. Understand that this is not how you are supposed to react. This is the time when your son really needs your help, and you must step up. An addiction is a problem that can be solved. However, you must be willing to act on it immediately and encourage your son to do the same. An addiction can effectively ruin your child's life. In this section, you will learn about certain practical tips that you can follow to help your son overcome these addictions.

Love him unconditionally

Teenagers test their parent's limits. They are quite adept at pushing their parent's buttons. Even under the best of times, they still do this. If you know that your teen is fighting an addiction, it will only get worse. As a parent, you must prepare yourself for some turbulence. There will be times when your teen tests your limits like never before. You must love your child unconditionally and show him that you do. This is one task you cannot take a break from. Your child must know that you love him regardless of addictions. If he feels like you don't love him, it will only worsen the situation. Battling addiction isn't easy and you must understand that your child will need a lot of support. In fact, he needs you now more than ever. He needs to know that he can count on you and that you will take care of him. You need to show him that he's loved even in the most trying situations. When he knows that he can count on you, his recovery will become easier.

A common mistake that a lot of parents tend to make is that they start treating their kid differently. Understand that your kid has a problem and that he needs your help to overcome it. If you start treating him like a stranger, they will feel unloved and the situation will likely worsen.

Self-care is important

Your parental instinct to protect your young one might kick in when you know that he is battling an addiction. You might be tempted to make combating his addiction your only priority. Yes, it must be your priority, but it must not be your only one. You don't have any mystical powers or a magic pill that can free him of his addiction. It is a process that he needs to face and overcome. You can certainly help him along the way, but you cannot do it all for him. Don't make the mistake of neglecting your life or your responsibilities to help your kid battle his addiction.

Don't forget that you need to live your life and take care of yourself too. If you don't do this, you will burn out. If this happens, you will be in no position to help your kid. You need to be healthy and strong right now. This is what your child needs. He needs someone to take care of him. If you can't even take care of your own mental and physical well-being, you will not be of much help to him.

Don't lose your cool

Keep your cool and maintain your composure. When you realize that your kid has some form of addiction, you might get angry. You might get quite angry, frustrated, and disappointed. These are powerful emotions, and you must keep them in check. Don't let these emotions get the best of you. You must respond and not react. Regardless of how tough it might be, you must keep your emotions in check. If you yell, shout, or even physically lash out at your child, it won't do anyone any good. It will make you feel guilty and worsen how your child is feeling.

Anger will only create more anger. If you want to handle the situation, then you need to stay calm. If you get angry, it will upset your teen and might also worsen his behavior. So, be an adult and stay calm.

Always listen

You must be a good listener. Now, more than ever is when your child really needs you. It is quintessential that you don't ignore the problem at hand. It is time to take action. However, the first step to do this is to start talking to your child. You need to talk to your teen about what his problem is and how the dependency started. It's not enough to just talk to him, but you must also listen to what he's saying. If you don't listen, then there is no point in having this conversation.

Understand that now is not the time to lecture him about anything. Believe it or not, your teen knows that he is in trouble. If you start lecturing him, you will only make him feel worse. All this can wait until he is better and has overcome his addiction. Be empathetic towards your child. He is hurting right now, and he needs you. He needs his parents and their support. Instead of indulging in a monologue, it is time to create a healthy dialogue. You must create an environment that is conducive of having such discussions. Listen to your teen without any judgment or criticism. All you need to do is listen. Once you start truly listening to him, you can discover his problem. It might also help you identify his triggers. You can ask a simple open-ended question and wait for his answer. There might be times when he doesn't want to talk to you so respect his wishes. Give him some space for a while. He will eventually get back to you. Don't force your child into starting a conversation that he clearly is not ready for. Avoid blaming him if he does say something.

Work together as a team

Never miss out on an opportunity to let your child know that you are a team. You and your child need to work together as a team. It is a good idea for all his loved ones to work together as a team and showcase a unified front. It gives him a lot of courage to know that he has a team of personal cheerleaders. Ensure that the environment in the house is peaceful and calm. If there are any domestic disturbances, then it will hamper your teen's recovery.

Don't enable him

You must never become an enabler. You must not enable him in any manner, either directly or indirectly. When you see your child in pain, you might want to solve his troubles. You might want to do everything you can to make this journey easy for him. Your parental instinct will certainly kick in, and you will want to do everything in your power to help him. However, in this bid to help him, you might end up doing more harm than good. If your teen is in trouble and you offer to help him all the time, he will become dependent on you. He might also start taking this for granted. I wouldn't be surprised if he starts believing that he can do whatever he wants, and his parents will clean up his mess.

Therefore, it is quintessential that you don't enable his behavior. Let him face the consequences of his addictions. You can support him and guide him along the way, but you must not clean up his mess. You can help him without being an enabler. You must stop yourself from doing anything that will give him a chance to continue his behavior. However, you can certainly do things to make the recovery process a little easier. So, if you know that your teen is abusing prescription medicine, then you must not give him any extra money.

Apart from all this, if you feel like you need additional help, then reach out. Don't hesitate to seek professional help. After all, this is about your child's well-being. You are not a miracle worker and don't put this burden on yourself. If you're unable to handle the situation and you know you need a little support, seek help. This will not only be helpful for your child, but it will be helpful to you as well.

CHAPTER THIRTEEN:

Dealing with ADHD, Anxiety, and Depression

Dealing with ADHD

Is your teen easily distracted, or does it seem like he cannot sit still? Does he often act impulsively and without thinking? Is he disorganized? Does he have frequent emotional outbursts? If yes, then it is quite likely that he has ADHD. A lot of parents are often embarrassed by such behavior of their kids even when they know that it is because of a disorder. Parenting a teen with ADHD is not easy. However, here are a couple of tips that you can use to make the process of parenting easier.

You must always live in the present. Don't live in the past and don't hold onto anything negative from the past. Deal with the current situation at hand. If your child does something wrong, then spare him the

"I told you" lectures. He doesn't need that right now. You can sit him down and talk to him about what he did wrong. But, don't resurface any issues from the past.

As a parent, you will obviously be compassionate toward your child. However, you might have to walk an extra mile when your child has ADHD. No one likes to be criticized, and the same stands true for your teen too. He wouldn't appreciate it if you constantly kept criticizing him about his behavior or if you kept blaming him. If your teen has ADHD, then it is quite likely that he will be disorganized and forgetful too. He isn't being disorganized to test your patience. It is just something that comes along with having ADHD. So, you must learn to be compassionate and understanding toward him. Also, your child might have little or no control over his impulses. However, you must not allow him to use his condition as an excuse to indulge in objectionable behavior. For instance, it is not okay for him to voluntarily engage in any wrong activity or behavior like shoplifting.

Being a parent isn't always easy. Perhaps one of the trickiest parts of parenting is the amount of patience it requires. There will be times when you are extremely upset, but you still need to keep your calm. So, while dealing with your kid, learn to stay calm. Getting into a shouting match with him will not do either of you any favors. Your approach to parenting might differ, but you must ensure that you keep your calm. It is a good idea to create a system of rules, along with reasonable consequences or penalties. You must not only create these rules but must also enforce them.

There will be certain pitfalls. You need to be able to anticipate the troubles your kid can get into and must have a solution to deal with those problems too. You must be proactive in your efforts to resolve any issues. Don't be under the misconception that it will always be smooth sailing. There will be good and bad days. So, prepare yourself. You must come up with ways in which you can constructively handle any trouble that your child gets into.

It is time to set certain limits. You must not only set certain limits but must adhere to them too. You must follow this rule when you are handing out any penalties. For instance, if you couldn't threaten him to eat his vegetables when he was five years old, you certainly cannot try the same tactic now. If you tell your kid that he is grounded for the rest of the year for not eating his veggies, it doesn't make any sense. Not only is this silly, but it isn't enforceable. So, the penalties you hand out must be reasonable and enforceable.

Appreciate the silver lining. Instead of harping on all the things that your child is doing wrong, it is time to focus on the things he's doing right. If he has managed to keep his room clean and organized for a month, don't forget to appreciate his efforts. Don't forget to appreciate or praise your teen whenever he does something good. Yes, he might do a couple of things wrong, but if you keep focusing only on his negative behavior, then it will make him resent you. Don't be a fault finder.

You must avoid getting into any power struggles. The best way to avoid getting into power struggles is by writing down rules. When you do this, you are effectively reducing the chances of any misunderstandings or ambiguity. Make a list of certain house rules along with the consequences of breaking those rules. These rules are not only applicable to him but are applicable to you as well. Another thing that you must keep in mind while making these rules is to consult your teen. For instance, you can withdraw his television privileges if he fails to perform satisfactorily at school. On the other hand, you will need to pay him or have some form of monetary compensation whenever he does any of the chores at home. So, you are rewarding good behavior while limiting undesirable behavior. Think of these rules as a contract that you must both abide by.

Teens with ADHD often find it difficult to interact socially with others. In fact, social interaction is something they are uncomfortable with, to begin with. So, it is time to talk to your teen about developing social skills. A couple of important social skills that he must develop include listening, holding a conversation, and not interrupting others while others are talking.

A teen with ADHD might find it difficult to express himself or his feelings. So, it is time to talk to him about this as well. You need to tell him that it is okay to express his feelings. Also, inform him that it is okay to feel whatever he feels. Encourage him to understand what he is feeling and how to express it. If your teen seems upset, then encourage him to talk about the things which have made him upset instead of carrying these emotions around. You can let your child vent his anger, but you need to set rules surrounding this. For instance, your child can rant as long as he doesn't use any profanity or doesn't get physical. Once he is done with his rant, you can tell him that you appreciate whatever he's told and that you will need a while to get back to him with advice. The only thing that you promised in the situation is a follow-up conversation and nothing more.

It is quintessential that you teach your child that a major offense will incur a serious penalty. You need to stand your ground on important issues. You need to be fair in the punishment you're doling out but ensure that the penalty justifies the misdeed committed. Once you have set certain rules, stand your ground. If you don't and give in, then your teen will understand that he can do as he pleases. The idea is to restrict risky behavior. Since teens who have ADHD tend to engage in risky behavior more than teens without ADHD, it is important to teach him the consequences of engaging in such behavior. Once he understands that indulging in risky behavior constitutes punishment, then he will stop acting in such a way. It can act as a deterrent. You need to have a zero-tolerance policy for any illegal or harmful activities that your kid can get into. High-risk behavior like using drugs, driving under the influence, or indulging in any harmful activities, must be discouraged. You need to talk to your teen about all these activities and the consequences at the same time. Once you tell him that if he doesn't stick to the rules, he will be punished, then stick to your statement.

You need to ensure that your teen has a healthy and nutritious diet. If his body doesn't get all the nourishment that he needs, then he will not be able to function optimally. If this happens, it will naturally increase your child's moodiness and irritability. So, it is a good idea to monitor his diet. Try limiting his intake of processed foods and sugars. Instead, replace all this with healthy and wholesome suits. Ensure that you have plenty of healthy snacks at home whenever your child gets angry. Make sure that he eats at least two or three healthy and nutritious meals at home every day.

It is time to start setting some boundaries. However, while you're setting any boundaries, take your teen's opinions into consideration. Give your teen a chance to express himself. Apart from this, start encouraging him to get involved in all such duties, which will help with his overall development.

Dealing with Anxiety

The feeling of experiencing butterflies in your stomach, or feeling tense is referred to as anxiety. We all tend to feel a little anxious from time to time. However, if your teen has an anxiety disorder, then he tends to experience these feelings constantly. Anxiety is your body's natural reaction to any challenging circumstances. Anxiety is rather common in teens. All the changes that they undergo in their teenage years, coupled with the fact that they will soon be adults can make them quite anxious. They are coming across opportunities and challenges that they weren't aware of until now. Any change can bring about anxiety, and becoming a teenager is certainly a major change for any kid.

For instance, he might be worried about starting at a new school or making new friends. He might also be worried about upcoming exams or public speaking. All these worries translate into anxiety. Anxiety isn't necessarily a bad thing. At times, it can help keep your teen safe and motivate them to excel. When left unchecked, it can become a disorder. Learning to manage anxiety and prevent it from getting the best of oneself is a very important life skill. If you know that your teen is experiencing anxiety, then the first thing you must do is tell him that it is okay. Tell him that it will go away with a little time. Also, encourage him to keep living his life without letting it hinder with any of his daily routines. Here are a couple of tips that you can follow to help your child deal with anxiety.

The first thing you must do is acknowledge that he is experiencing anxiety. The sooner you acknowledge the problem, the easier it will be to help remedy it. Your child must know that you are taking him seriously and that his emotions are valid. If you don't believe him, then he will not open up to you. Apart from this, he also needs to know that he has your full support. You can start encouraging your child to slowly start engaging in all those activities that make him anxious. For instance, let us assume that your son is scared of public speaking. To help overcome this fear, encourage him to prepare a speech that he can deliver in front of you, then in front of his friends or his loved ones. After a while, he will gain confidence in his public speaking abilities and he will overcome his anxiety. However, don't rush him into anything that he isn't ready for yet.

Don't make a fuss if your child refuses to do something because of his anxiety. You need to give him the confidence to overcome his anxiety. However, if you start lecturing him or make a big deal about it, then you will only worsen his anxiety. So, stay calm and instead talk to him about it. Tell him that it is okay if he doesn't want to do something in the moment. Also, tell him that you know that he has the ability to manage his feelings. Don't make him feel like he is making a mistake. Instead, encourage him to take steps to help overcome his anxiety.

You need to encourage your child to start exploring his worries and fears. Once he starts talking about his fears, you might be able to understand why he has those fears. As you identify the cause, it becomes easier to tackle the situation. Encourage your child to express himself.

Dealing with Depression

It is okay to feel sad at times. However, if this feeling prolongs for longer than necessary, then it might be a sign of depression. Depression has become quite common in teens these days. Depression can make your teen feel dejected and unmotivated. Apart from this, it will constantly hamper his ability to be happy. It will also take a toll on his overall well-being. In this section, you will learn about a couple of simple tips that you can follow to help your child overcome depression.

The first step in helping your teen deal with depression is to talk to him about his feelings. He might admit what he's feeling if you talk with him. It will not only lighten his burden, but it will also make him feel better. Keep your calm and don't criticize anything that your son says. You need to listen to him. If you feel like he might have any tendency to harm himself, then seek professional help immediately.

Let your son know that you love him and will support him regardless of what he feels. So, encourage him to start embracing his feelings. Not just embracing his feelings but also expressing them. If your teen feels sad, ask him to express himself. Discourage him from bottling up all his emotions within.

You must consult your teen's doctor about his depression as well. There are certain medications that can lead to depression. So, talk to his doctor and if possible, change such medications.

Encourage him to spend more time outdoors. If he spends a lot of his time with his peers or others who make him happy, his mood will improve immediately. Also, encourage him to spend more time doing things that he loves. If he likes to paint, then encourage him to paint, and get him new supplies too.

Ensure that he has a healthy balanced diet. Also, make sure that there is some form of physical activity included in his daily routine. A combination of these factors will not only improve your sleep cycle but will also uplift his mood. If he has an athletic side to him, then motivate him to take up a team sport. The more time he spends with like-minded people, the better he will feel.

Ensure that you try limiting the stress that he experiences. The more stressed he feels, the more depressed he will likely be. Apart from this, make sure that your house is a safe and secure environment. There is nothing unnatural about depression and talking about mental health isn't a taboo subject anymore. So, start talking to your teen about all of this.

Conclusion

I want to thank you once again for choosing this book. I hope it proved to be an informative and entertaining read.

Raising a teenage boy isn't always a cakewalk. There will be times where you will feel frustrated, angry, or even disappointed. Likewise, there will be times when it feels like it is impossible to talk to your child. You might not know what to do and might feel helpless. However, all of this can be easily remedied. You don't have to feel helpless or overwhelmed while parenting your teenage son. It is easy if you are willing to make a couple of changes.

By now, you would have realized that you must change your parenting style as your child grows older. You must start giving your kid the freedom he desires while setting certain reasonable restrictions. You need to connect and communicate with him to avoid any conflicts. You must have all those awkward conversations about sex and mental health. You need to start treating your son like an adult if you want him to behave like one. Phew, that was a lot. However, it can all be easily accomplished. When in doubt, refer to this book. This book will act as your guide as you wade through your son's teenage years.

Now, all that's left for you to do is start following the simple tips and tricks given in this book to strengthen the bond with your teenager. It can be done, but remember to be patient, empathetic, and loving along the way.

Thank you and all the best!

References:

12 Essential Tips for Positive Parenting Your Teen Cherishing your Baby. (2019). Retrieved from https://www.ahaparenting.com/Ages-stages/teenagers/parenting-teens

Adolescent Depression: What Parents Can Do To Help. (2019). Retrieved from https://www.healthychildren.org/English/health-issues/conditions/emotional-problems/Pages/Childhood-Depression-What-Parents-Can-Do-To-Help.aspx

Conflict management with teenagers. (2019). Retrieved from https://raisingchildren.net.au/teens/communicating-relationships/communicating/conflict-management-with-teens

Dealing with Troubled Teens: A 7-Step Guide for Parents. (2019). Retrieved from https://drugabuse.com/dealing-troubled-teens/

Fader, S. (2018). 18 Areas Of Normal Adolescent Behavior | Betterhelp. Retrieved from https://www.betterhelp.com/advice/adolescence/18-areas-of-normal-adolescent-behavior/

Goins, J. 3 Ways Parents Can Help Their Children Find Their Calling. Retrieved from https://www.focusonthefamily.com/parenting/parenting-challenges/3-ways-parents-can-help-their-children-find-their-calling

Gould, S. (2019). 8 Ways to Connect With Your Teen Son When He Won't Talk to You. Retrieved from https://momsoftweensandteens.com/how-can-i-get-my-teenage-boy-to-talk/

How to Deal with Your Teenage Son: Tips for Parents | Newport Academy. (2018). Retrieved from https://www.newportacademy.com/resources/restoring-families/how-to-deal-with-your-teenage-son/

How To Speak To Your Teenage Son - 10 Parent Tips - Ditch the Label. (2017). Retrieved from https://www.ditchthelabel.org/10-tips-parents-speak-teenage-son/

Independence in teenagers: how to support it. (2019). Retrieved from https://raisingchildren.net.au/pre-teens/development/social-emotional-development/independence-in-teens

Mersch, J. (2019). 13 Tips for Parenting a Teen With ADHD: Get Strategies. Retrieved from https://www.medicinenet.com/13_tips_for_parenting_a_teen_with_adhd/article.htm#introduction_to_parenting_teens

Mweseni, S. (2018). 6 ways that parenting styles have changed over time - AfroMum. Retrieved from http://www.afromum.com/6-ways-parenting-styles-changed-time/

Poole, D. (2017). 5 Tips for Talking to Your Teenager About Mental Health. Retrieved from https://www.mentalhealthfirstaid.org/2017/06/5-tips-talking-teenager/

Rafferty, J. (2019). Gender Identity Development in Children. Retrieved from https://www.healthychildren.org/English/ages-stages/gradeschool/Pages/Gender-Identity-and-Gender-Confusion-In-Children.aspx

Vinderine, S. (2015). HuffPost is now a part of Oath. Retrieved from https://m.huffingtonpost.ca/sharon-vinderine/best-parenting-style_b_8582564.html

Young, K. (2019). Anxiety in Teens - How to Help a Teenager Deal With Anxiety. Retrieved from https://www.heysigmund.com/anxiety-in-teens/

Made in the USA
Middletown, DE
23 August 2019